JUST TELL ME WHAT TO DO

Just Tell Me What To Do

LAUREN MICHELE FIELDS

This book is not intended as a substitute for the medical recommendations of mental health professionals. Instead, it is intended to provide insights that encourage readers to collaborate with mental health professionals and other experts in their pursuit of optimal well-being.

These are memories, from my perspective, and I have tried to represent events as faithfully as possible.

www.laurenmichelefields.com

ISBN 979-8-9920896-0-8
Library of Congress Control Number: 2024925589

E-book ISBN 979-8-9920896-1-5

*For the version of me
who waited patiently
to be seen.*

CONTENTS

Preface

The dismantling of my life, on the surface, took exactly two years—from the day my ex-husband and I stepped into a therapist's office to the day I received my last paycheck after walking away from a twenty-year career. But the cracks started to show much earlier, in my mid-thirties. My marriage to my high-school sweetheart, spanning nearly two decades, hit yet another cycle of "we hate each other." My body began doing mysterious and insufferable things. My two wonderful, overly-scheduled children continued to consume most of my energy and time and were now old enough to change the dynamic of the house. Meanwhile, my demanding career—climbing a ladder that I had been told I wanted to climb—was giving me panic attacks. I had a nagging sense that the tolerable misery I had sustained until then wasn't going to hold much longer.

Fast-forward five dramatically disruptive years, and I was laying the final piece of my old life to rest. I had left my marriage and embarked on a deeply independent, heart-healing journey. I had completely revamped my home, my hobbies, my finances, and my time. I had nurtured my relationship with my now-teenage children and eliminated most of my other relationships. I had begun a complete health overhaul and eventually reached a breaking point in my job. I hadn't intended to quit when I began dismantling everything else. In fact, my career had absorbed my entire identity after I left the codependency of my marriage. But the more I worked on finding and loving myself, the more my anger went away. Then it became clear: my job was just another version of the things I had already cut from my life—a light-dimming, growth-limiting, chaotic environment where I poured all my energy into creating dreams for others while abandoning my own. Work had become another place that triggered my core wounds. The transformative healing I was doing in my personal life brought a new perspective on my professional one.

It took about six months from this realization to burn out completely. Nothing had changed—except me. I had to face the fact that I had outgrown my entire old life, even my job. This was hard to accept. Relationships were one thing; they involved other people. But work—that had been all me. I had once derived all my validation from my career, and now I couldn't even pull into the parking lot without breaking down. After fourteen years at this company and twenty in the industry, it was time for a change.

After some promising initial conversations, I was buzzing with newfound energy. Maybe I *could* make this move. My practical mind told me to not leave until I had secured the next thing. Early in my career, I had quit a job and moved across the state without another lined up—it had seemed like a terrible decision at the time (it wasn't). Plus, now I was a single mother. I had no one to rely on but myself. The problem was, my gut wanted me out *now*. My tolerance of frustration was at rock bottom.

A financial plan could bridge the gap. I brainstormed scenarios, factoring in bonus money, my budget, and savings to give myself permission to quit. It penciled out. Then, after one more promising conversation about a new opportunity, I decided: the hell with it. I didn't think the net would appear unless I jumped first. So I did—although it felt more like the universe pushed me.

Leaving was equal parts terrifying and freeing. I had been so fixated on what I didn't want, I couldn't identify what I did. Then the word hit me: freedom. I wanted total control over my life—my time, my money, my emotional stability, all of it. I was burnt out from trying to have it all. I didn't want it all. I wanted the freedom to figure out what I did want. The high of the first few days at home was intoxicating. It felt like I was playing hooky from life—deliriously fun, yet the looming "future" made it impossible to fully relax.

I had a meeting with a potential opportunity, and three sentences in, I knew it wasn't going to work out. The more I sat there, the faster I realized this felt too much like what I'd just left—a place where I'd surely abandon myself again. After a few more calls, I had an existential crisis. None of this felt right. My whole body screamed that finding another job, or even going out on my own, was not what I wanted. I had jumped, but instead of a net, a brick wall had appeared, and it was telling me this was not it.

I'm a huge believer in intuition, and when I'd trusted mine before, it had always been right. My problem was, I had spent most of my life stubbornly ignoring it, making decisions with my head while my heart was completely disconnected. But this time, my intuition wasn't giving me a choice. I knew that anything resembling my old life was not an option. Okay, fine. But what the hell do I do now?

I did what any slightly OCD over-thinker would do: I made another budget. I had given myself a buffer, but what if I could stretch it further? I roughed out the math, ruminated over my lifestyle, and scheduled a meeting with my financial advisor. I had a lot on my side: a successful twenty-year career, a divorce that had stopped the faucet of spending, (we spent because we hated each other), a big bonus, and a small inheritance I'd nurtured for years. All of this had left me in a prime position. I stretched my financial situation to sustain me for twice the time I'd originally planned, leaving me with the thing I had prayed for: time.

With temporary financial freedom, I gave up trying to figure it all out immediately. After all, there's no playbook for a forty-one-year-old woman deciding what comes next. Once you age out of the whole "get married and have kids" rhetoric, society deems you useless. Too old to be hot, too young to be wise, too experienced to stay quiet, and too burnt out to give a damn. Render me a menace. There were people out there doing what I was searching for; I just couldn't find them. And the ones who came close usually lost me with, "And then I found the love of my life." Ugh. Fairy tales really messed us up. My happily-ever-after wasn't at the top of a corporate ladder or the other end of a dating app. There had to be more to life than corporate greed and getting validation from a partner I hadn't gotten from my parents. I was desperate for answers—a roadmap. *Someone, just tell me what to do.*

I realized I needed rest—real rest. I had been caught in constant motion, burned out from years of pretending to have it all. My body needed time to recover from a lifetime of running at full speed. I knew I'd eventually find my way, so I made a decision: this summer, I would stop doing and simply live in joy. I wanted to savor time with my kids, embrace my own peace and freedom, and dive deeper into the healing that had already begun. What followed was a transformative summer—a profound journey of self-discovery, healing, and change. It became clear that despite how much I'd evolved, I was still tethered to old belief systems. Dismantling my life wasn't enough; it would take intentional action to change my thoughts and behavior patterns. By the end of the summer, I felt a seismic shift in how I viewed everything. I had fundamentally changed.

After the kids went back to school, I spent the day with a friend I hadn't seen since I'd left my job. As we shared stories about our summers and the similar questions we faced about what was next, she validated something I had sensed all along: I had curated a framework of methods and exercises that could help others. I knew I wasn't alone in this longing for realignment and clarity. It had been on my mind all summer. I couldn't be alone in wanting someone to just tell me what to do, give me an example, show me their work. Everything I had devoured over the summer had been miraculous in some way, but it was all so specific. I didn't want a twelve-week course on just one thing. It felt burdensome to chase it all. Courses for connecting to spirit, classes on somatic healing, workshops on the law of attraction, books about reframing, career coaches, etc. I needed a sampler—different tools that could be personalized for maximum impact, and I needed it *now* because I get excited like that. At the end of our day together, my friend confirmed what I felt. "You're exuding happiness and positivity in a way that feels new and different," she said. I smiled. "I know. I feel like a completely different person."

I felt ready, finally, to live the life I was always meant to live—with my whole self. I found the missing pieces. I crafted tools that helped me shift my belief systems. I learned lessons that replaced old conditioning, and I addressed wounds and traumas. I turned a life I used to be embarrassed by into one I'm not afraid to love. And now I'm excited at the idea that someone out there might benefit from this too.

This book is for those who are already well along their self-love journey— past the affirmations and self-care routines, but still feeling the weight of the final barriers. If you've burned away much of your old life, or if you recognize you're repeating patterns that no longer serve you, this is for you. Maybe it's level two, maybe it's level ten, but there was a decade of self-help and actual help that got me ready for the deep transformation that took place this summer. If you're there, think of this book as my course notes, handed to you to speed up your learning.

I'll be sharing the framework that helped me craft a cathartic season of healing, leveraging the skills I'd already developed while just trying to survive, along with my personal story. I encourage you to continue exploring content that resonates with you—read the experts, take the classes, listen to the podcasts. This book is a nudge to help you make the change more efficient. I'm fortunate to have had the time and resources to immerse myself in this journey, but everything I did can be adapted to fit your unique life. My goal is to inspire you to create your own season of healing, uncovering truths you already know.

This book reads linearly, but healing rarely is. I've organized what I learned in a general order, but much of the process felt like a spiral, with lessons overlapping. If something doesn't resonate with you right now, skip ahead to what does. Trust that the path will make sense in time, and the more you listen to yourself, the more you'll be on the right track. I've found that a hundred small things, done consistently, work more magic than one big thing.

I want us all to find that magic.

PART 1

| 1 |

Context

You're joining this story close to the end because that's where the real gold is. I could tell you about my "perfect on paper" life, or the five years of last straws that led to my divorce. I could detail the workbook that got me through it, share the joy of dancing in my kitchen, or recount a steamy rendezvous in the middle of the day. I could tell you about that time I tried hot yoga or the solo trip where I cried on the plane and spotted a celebrity without her hair extensions (not the reason I cried). I could even share how I approached meeting my ex's new girlfriend for coffee before she met my kids or what self-help books and podcasts shaped my journey. I could detail how I did three burn buckets under the full moon and hosted a yard sale on my wedding anniversary. But those stories are just the beginning, and they don't capture the essence of what I encountered this summer.

What is important are two poignant moments that shook me into my awakening. The first was when my daughter, my oldest, reached the age where she began navigating more complex social situations. As the discussions shifted from general politeness and courtesy to deeper lessons about interpersonal relationships, I began to feel anxious. Eventually, I knew the advice I was giving her—based on what I thought I wanted for her—didn't align with how I was managing my own life. As we moved further into this stage of life, I realized I had been coaching her on things I needed coaching on myself.

I remember one day having a heart-to-heart with her on how she deserved respect from others and it was her right not to accept anything less. I could feel myself choking on those words. I knew them to be true, but was overwhelmed by the shame of not practicing what I preached. I realized that anything I said was fleeting, and what she was really watching was what I did.

That conversation was a mirror and a spotlight I couldn't ignore. I had to admit that I wasn't living a life I'd want for my child and hadn't even noticed what I had been doing to myself. The lesson was mine to learn. That day opened my eyes to all the places my intent and my behavior didn't align, sending me down a path of revelation that eventually led to the lawyer's office.

The second soul-shifting moment was at the end of an argument with my then-husband. The pressure of the relationship had built up again, and we were at each other's throats, releasing months of bottled-up resentment. The typical cycle of repress, explode, express, ignore was rearing its head. We had been together so long that that cycle of misery felt comfortable and, dare I say it, normal. But for some reason, this fight was different. It wasn't bigger or worse, or even about anything memorable—just the usual attack on each other for unmet needs. But something happened to me in that moment. I remember sitting on my couch as he decided it was time to retreat from the argument (something I never did—digging in my heels was my specialty). I had this moment of clarity and said to myself, "I am not this hard to love."

That realization shifted something in me, and I finally believed something I hadn't before. I wasn't needy or difficult. I wasn't asking for anything outside of what I would give to someone else. In that moment, I decided I was lovable, and it changed everything. I stopped begging for someone who clearly didn't like me to please love me. And my world shifted.

It was these and a hundred other moments that had me asking myself if I was stuck in some sort of surface satisfaction with my life. When I wasn't breaking down, it was still miserable—but tolerable. I could go through the motions, but eventually I realized actual joy, gratitude, and happiness were fleeting.

Thousands of women are leaving bad marriages, relationships, and jobs, realizing that the bar for others is set on the floor, while the one we live by is unattainable. We're waking up to the mental load we carry and the fact that we've been doing it alone all along. There are countless accounts of it being easier without the dead weight of a spouse, and tons of articles about the bait-and-switch of becoming a wife and the toll it takes on women today. While I'm grateful for those resources—and I used many to find my way—this story is from after all of that.

Here I sit, on my screened-in porch in East Coast suburbia, several years into this healing, ready to share the second part of my journey—a summer of rapid personal growth and deep internal transformation. I'm here to show you how I got to the root of the issues that made me want to leave everything, and I shifted who I am enough to find the path to alignment—leaving my old limiting patterns and beliefs behind. I've befriended my trauma and turned it into a catalyst of personal awakening.

I'm not a world traveler. I wasn't in a cool band. I'm not related to a celebrity. I don't live or work in a big city. I'm not in tech. I don't want to live in LA. I didn't go to an Ivy League school or obtain a handful of advanced degrees. I'm not from a one-light town in the Midwest. I'm just someone who fits into the average demographic targets.

I've been gaslit and emotionally abused. I've been shamed for having interests that weren't cool, minimized to fit someone else's aesthetic, lied to, and abandoned. I've been criticized and second-guessed, making every major decision for my family while second-guessing myself the entire time. I've been reprimanded in the guise of "jokes." And I've found happiness and self-love on the other side of a toxic relationship.

I convinced myself I found purpose in work, needing to hit milestones by specific ages. I pushed hard and fast to earn and produce and show that I was valuable enough for mediocre men to keep around. I studied, crammed, and faked it to keep advancing—seeking more and more validation. I spoke, trained, made decisions, advised, coached, mentored, and shouldered the emotional burdens of less-adjusted colleagues. I did everything I was asked—and more—because that's what it takes to stay in the game.

I observed the game, studied it, and played it to exhaustion. I abandoned my true self, using my femininity only when tolerated, and sank so deep into my masculine energy that once, a mentor told me my boss thought of me as "one of the guys." I took it as a compliment. I only talked about motherhood when it advanced my status, keeping my likes, desires, and hobbies to myself.

I've climbed the career ladder as a small fish in a big pond and then a big fish in a small one. I've been catcalled on job sites, been instructed to flirt with decision-makers, and been called "sweetheart" at work too many times (more than zero). I've been mistaken for an assistant when I was the boss, delegated as the note-taker, and gaslit into thinking my project management skills were simply "being organized." I've had to prove my worth before promotion, sitting next to men with no experience but "potential." I've been told I'm too bossy, too quiet, too direct, too nice. I've been told I look angry when I'm not actively smiling. I've had people take credit for my work. I've been the only woman at the table, pretending to like golf, beer, and football to stay in the conversation. I've sat at executive tables where everyone but me had a stay-at-home wife.

I could recount every frustrating detail that led to my final goodbye—how many times I cried in my car or had panic attacks in the bathroom. I could detail the last straw and then the last-last straw. I could tell you how many times I justified the money and then how I missed something for my kids because of a late meeting or traffic on my commute home. I could tell you the moment I realized I loved myself more than I craved false validation. But none of that actually matters. Eventually, we all find ourselves on the other side, whether by choice or by being shoved by higher forces. What matters is what we do after we decide to stop standing in the fire. I'm tired of chasing, fighting, manipulating, amending, shapeshifting, and minimizing. I am exhausted. There is a better way, and I'm tired of us not knowing it.

I'm only special in the way that we're all special—which is to say I fit squarely in the average bucket. I'm a middle-aged woman, a former "A" student, who followed the rules and did everything I was "supposed" to do. I believed the messages promising that if I was a "good girl," I'd get everything I wanted (and deserved). I crossed my t's and dotted my i's, picked up others' slack, cleaned up the messes left behind. I made everything nice and presentable, learned to perform for praise, choked down my intuition and feelings for the sake of teamwork, and showed up when I so desperately wanted to retreat. I pushed myself through exhaustion, ignored signs of burnout, sacrificed my needs to be a good mother, wife, and employee, and waited patiently for my reward.

Then one day, I decided that could all go fuck itself. My breaking point came from the cumulative effect of a million small cuts—looking around at my life and realizing everything was just off enough for me to be completely in the wrong place. Once I started dismantling it all, it became addicting. I didn't stop until I was stripped to the bone. I knew I wanted something else, but had no clue what.

My point is, I'm probably you—maybe older, younger, or just farther along. I'm learning things others have already discovered. I'm one of the masses buying products, following trends, trying the newest tip, trick, and hack to make it all go—swaying in the winds of culture and consumerism. Like so many others, I'm waking up in midlife, with two kids at home and a mortgage, asking myself what the hell I'm waiting for.

I'm not doing van life (not my vibe), not moving to an island, not backpacking through Europe. I'm not an influencer, a savant, an undiscovered talent. I'm just a woman in the suburbs of Pennsylvania, going to soccer games and the grocery store, trying to live a profoundly simple, boring, and extraordinary life.

All of this to say, I hope you find so much of yourself in my story that it's a little scary.

| 2 |

Solitude

Every self-help book I'd ever read made me feel like there was something wrong with me for not having a go-to person or people. Each story had its own spouse, siblings, mentor, or best-friend as the stable supporting character to the main character's journey. But that wasn't me. I hadn't healed enough to attract securely attached people into my life, and I hadn't healed enough to believe I even deserved them.

I've never had a big support system. I don't have much family, and the ones I do have, I'm not close with. I lost my mother at a young age, which shattered any sense of safety that comes from a reliable maternal figure. I had a handful of friends, but I hadn't done a great job nurturing those relationships. I hadn't made a new friend in decades and wasn't great at keeping up with the ones I had. This hit me hardest when faced with filling out the Emergency Contact section of documents, or when updating my will—I struggled to find an executor until my kids came of age. The emptiness was a reminder of the fear I had around starting this journey.

Early in my post-divorce life, I read that human connection is essential to existence, and I felt overcome—again—with shame and frustration about how solitary my life was. I was tired of feeling disposable and invisible.

I pulled out my notebook and drew a graphic to understand what I wanted from relationships. I sketched concentric circles, labeling them with levels of closeness: soul mate, best friends, good friends, acquaintances, and obligations. Then I filled in names of people from my life. The exercise brought several important realizations: I wasn't as alone as I thought. It was okay to have open spaces. It was normal, even healthy, for people to shift between circles. Relationships change, and that's natural—it doesn't make any of them less meaningful. I also realized I had to release unrealistic expectations for some relationships and let them be what they were. I had never considered that an obligatory relationship didn't deserve the same time and energy as a best friend. I had also never considered that I was the decision-maker in where the names went.

This clarity showed me where I was lacking and what that meant for moving forward. I wasn't interested in collecting more acquaintances; I craved deeper connections. Either the relationships I desired already existed and needed to be nurtured, or I had to engage differently to meet the kinds of people who could fill those spaces. Most importantly, I placed myself at the center of my relationships instead of waiting to be accepted into someone else's circle.

I'm not a joiner. I hate groups. I love one-on-one connections, real conversations. I'd rather exchange names and deep stories than engage in small talk. I find surface-level interactions draining, and I want to be invited without the pressure of attending, just so I feel included. So much of the advice about connection and community annoyed me. While I agree that connection is essential, I also believe there are other ways to achieve it—ways that don't require depending on others, signing up for things, and "putting yourself out there" (my worst nightmare).

As I prepared to leave my job, I spent thoughtful time disconnecting my identity from that place and the relationships I had built. In team meetings, I'd think, "Take this all in; this is the last time you'll be here." Or, "Be proud of what you've accomplished; it's time to close this chapter." I knew leaving would strip me down to a skeleton crew of people left in my life, but I wanted to avoid being triggered by it all over again.

After I had left, I received many very thoughtful messages and calls. Each message was similar—I'm so sad that you're leaving, I'm so grateful for the time together—I know you'll kill it in whatever you do next—let's keep in touch. Hard yes for all of those, but it had me thinking. I'm glad these people were so confident in my ability to figure out what was next—but I wasn't there yet. I searched in each conversation for clues to what that should be. These people knew me, worked with me, observed me. It felt like they were more qualified to tell me what to do next than I was.

None of those answers came. And as I let the professional relationships fade away into "keep in touch," I knew that work Lauren had to die too. Parts of her would stay with me, but the person I had become to thrive in that environment was not the person I would be moving forward.

The first decision I made was that the healing and discovery I embarked on this summer would be a solo journey. My abandonment issues had already been triggered by leaving my marriage, but finding the courage to be alone was a major step in preparing for divorce. After two years of living with a custody schedule that left my house routinely quiet, I had come to terms with what *alone* really meant—and surprisingly, I found peace in it. Having grown up as an only child, I was able to rediscover the love I had for my own company.

Heading into this summer, I let go of all the things I'd been told about connection. I knew there was a risk I could slip into a deep depression, but I decided it was worth it. Forcing myself into groups or into spaces where I didn't feel comfortable was no longer an option. I was determined to trust myself, to figure this out on my own. Maybe my hyper-independence was an overcorrection for the codependent/people-pleasing tendencies I had developed as a trauma response—but I didn't care. This was the path I needed to take.

I cleared my schedule. I only said yes to invitations that felt like a full-body yes. I settled into my solitude and finally committed to facing it head-on, embracing it.

| 3 |

New Energy

I might have been home, but my body was still in corporate mode. I didn't know yet how to turn it off. I was still getting calls from people learning I had left and a handful of well-meaning check-ins asking how my time off was. I still felt like I should be performing—but now as a productive unemployed person. I had felt a little like this when I had first announced my divorce—like I was being studied as a social experiment. The people who knew, watching my every move, putting themselves in my shoes, looking for successes and failures to justify their own situations. I felt compelled to produce, to be ecstatic, to do all of the things I had always dreamed about if I ever won the lottery and said goodbye to work forever. It was a lot of pressure, and I was disoriented. So I did what any good little performer would do—I dove into my chores.

The freedom of my single life had me consistently clearing out old energy. By the summer, I had already repainted, purged, and rearranged the furniture. I had switched from millennial grey to vibrant splashes of color, adding florals, textures, and life back into my home. I loved every part of my house now. It was my sanctuary. I didn't want to overhaul the whole house again, but I knew another kind of purge was in order to support the deeper insights I was seeking. This time, I decided to focus on my mental load.

What were the things that lived in my mind under the heading, "When I have time, I'll get to this?" Clean the garage. Set up the porch for summer. Reimagine my home office. Perfect—a task list.

The truth is, I had believed for so long that my worth was tied to what I could produce. Even though I had followed my intuition straight into unemployment, my self-worth had been triggered again. If I didn't have something to do or something to show for my effort, I felt like I might fall apart. I had just committed to slowing down and listening, and here I was jumping right into tasks. Old habits are hard to break—but it wasn't going to happen overnight.

Cleaning became the perfect starting point. Movement is paramount for self-discovery, and cleaning creates both physical and mental space. It also helps shift the energy of a place, making room for change. Even though I wasn't fully aware of my underlying belief about productivity and self-worth, I would still reap the benefits of the process along the way.

Two big tasks stood out: clean the garage and scrub the back porch. The garage had been nagging at me for months—every time I saw it, I felt guilt about not getting it done. So, I committed a full day to tackle it, but surprisingly finished in three hours. I cleared everything: organized, tossed, donated, and even rehoused some spiders. The key here was not getting sidetracked by other projects—I shockingly stayed focused on what would make me feel good when I walked into the space.

Next, I deep-cleaned the back porch. With summer approaching, I wanted to spend more time outdoors, so I made sure it was as clean and inviting as the inside of my home. This took two days, and despite the rain, I felt like the earth was cheering me on. It was a cleansing process on every level. Music, favorite drinks, and breaks to eat were essential to keep the flow going. And I took several progress pictures for that satisfying sense of accomplishment.

JUST TELL ME WHAT TO DO - 15

Cleaning, for me, is transformative. It gets my body moving, and as I decluttered my space, I found my mind clearing too. I kept a journal handy and paused many times to capture ideas and inspiration. Cleaning is as much about mental clarity as it is about physical space.

Once I tackled those two major tasks, other areas in my home started to call for attention. I had found flow—when I started aligning my spaces with what felt good, I naturally noticed what was still out of alignment. I was happy with the progress.

Next up was my home office. This room had held so much of my old life—my career, my past identities showing up on all my old business cards. I needed it to reflect who I was becoming, so I spent time just being in the space, allowing it to reveal how it wanted to feel. I put on music and spun around in my office chair to lighten the mood. It was hard to let go of these old accomplishments—like I was throwing parts of me away. Eventually, I settled on the word "complete." I had completed that journey, that learning, those relationships. Completing it let me be ready to start what comes next. Suddenly, the weight of grief became light with love. I purged old work notes, tossed company swag, and rearranged artwork. The goal was to create a neutral, refreshing environment, open for whatever came next.

As I continued to purge, I cleared out other lingering tasks: clothes to donate, frames I hadn't hung, random piles that had been ignored for months. Finally, I did an energetic cleanse of the space and rearranged some crystals to lock in the fresh, new energy.

This phase of decluttering was about more than just cleaning; it was about shedding old identities and creating space for the new. It was a powerful and necessary first step in aligning my external world with my internal growth. A deep cleaning for deep insights.

MAKING SPACE

The biggest change that came with leaving my job was deleting my inbox. It was the most notable, jarring, and liberating change. That mind-eating gremlin, with its incessant red notification bubble, kept my world in constant chaos—everything unfinished, an infinite "to do" list, and the anxiety over the next problem waiting to drop. I even had phantom notifications for days. Eventually, my brain started to reset, and the quiet began to settle in. This was bliss. I remembered, *yes*, it was quiet I had been seeking. Without the constant distraction of other people's problems to solve, I might finally be able to hear my own. I knew I had to maximize this feeling. So, I went on a mission—not only would I limit what came to me, but I would also curate what I allowed in.

My new mantra became: unsubscribe, block, mute, delete. The silence of not having a work inbox needed to spill into my personal email. I questioned, "What do people even need to email me for?" I wanted it to be a tool for intentional communication, not a dumping ground for marketing campaigns. So, I did a big unsubscribe.

Next, I turned to my apps. Anything I didn't actively use, I deleted. I reorganized my home screen to reflect how I wanted to spend my time, being mindful of what stayed front and center. Months earlier, I had changed my grouped app labels to affirmations after seeing it suggested online. I reviewed them again for alignment. For example: my streaming apps became "I am entertained," my photos and editing apps, "I am creative," and health and wellness apps, "I am healthy." It may sound small, but these affirmations became powerful.

With the clutter gone, I set an intention for social media. I wanted it to foster positive connections with people I valued but wouldn't normally see. I'd done something similar after the divorce—disconnecting from people who no longer needed access to me. It took time, but I eventually curated a list of connections that brought me joy, not stress. Fifty meaningful connections felt far better than two hundred who triggered judgment or anxiety.

I checked myself on celebrity and brand follows and cleared out anything that looked like the old version of me. If I ignored their content, I deleted them. If there was someone I didn't like, I deleted them. If I was judging myself because of what they would post, I deleted them. My intention for following accounts became: things that bring me joy, make me laugh, inspire me, or educate me.

My feed is now funny memes (mostly puns), artists who post about their work and the process of their work, doctors who talk about peri-menopause and menopause (not the fear-mongering ones), nutritionists, my favorite pop music girlies, my favorite women's sports teams, and my kids' school and sports organizations. The algorithm does the rest. Social media, like food, is either medicine or poison. There is no neutral.

This helped me purge my podcasts, books, shows, and movies too. I watch reality TV. It helps me understand human behavior. I don't watch all of it, but I love some of it. If I start it and it makes me feel bad, I turn it off. I love sci-fi and dystopian future stuff. Horror, forget it. And I'm like the only middle-aged woman who can't do true crime. There are no collective rights and wrongs. There is still a place for contrast and emotional depth, but I am mindful about how it fits into my day and the emotions it brings up.

Now the big one, music. I learned that music is manifesting, and the things I sing must be aligned with who I want to be. I thought back to the spring when my son complained, on the way to a soccer tournament, "Mom, no sad songs." I protested, "Most songs are about deep things!" He rolled his eyes, and we switched to a more upbeat station. Later, my daughter pointed out that whenever we asked Alexa to play music, we always got a compilation of intense songs. "Does Alexa think we're depressed?" she asked. We still laugh about it. But maybe that was the point. Was I just feeding into my misery with what I was consuming? With that said, I didn't want to delete my "sad girl autumn" playlist, so I didn't. But I added two new ones focused on positive messages and affirmations.

I favorited a few stations on my streaming service—Meditation, Yoga, Classical—for background music. I curated two specific playlists, Manifest and Healing Frequencies, to use when necessary. Nothing has shaken me out of a self-sabotage session like my Manifest playlist. Singing words about how awesome I am or my immense gratitude immediately reprograms my brain, and suddenly, the thing I was drowning in, is just gone. These took time to get them where I wanted, but they are so worth it. I didn't touch any of my other playlists. I still have playlists that got me through some stuff, but I really never find myself even wanting to listen to those. I look at them now fondly as reminders of how far I've come. Music has been one of the most powerful tools I've used to change my own mindset and behavior.

These activities were all about being intentional with my attention. I knew that whatever I focused on would shape my life. Simple choices—like curating what I look at, listen to, and watch each day—were essential in creating the change I was craving.

PART 2

| 4 |

Permission to Play

Two weeks before I quit my job, a colleague of mine texted me a book recommendation—*The Artist's Way at Work*, by Julia Cameron. This person occasionally sent me recommendations like this. I had a lot going on mentally, so I pinned it for a later time. The day I resigned, I ran into her in the lobby of our central office. Her office was forty-five minutes away, but she had stopped in to see our IT team. It had been the only ninety seconds I had stepped outside of my office all morning. Still distracted by the life-changing decision I was in the midst of, I mostly ignored the serendipity of the encounter. Two days later, I saw a video on my feed about the original *The Artist's Way* book and finally I paid attention. *This message keeps coming into my orbit, and now I have the time; maybe it's time to pick it up.* The funny thing is, I had the book already. My therapist had recommended it to me a year prior. I had bought it back then but never opened it. So, the day after I finished my porch cleaning, I grabbed the book, found the perfect sun-soaked spot outside, and started reading.

I'm not exaggerating when I say this book instantly changed my life. I had never felt more of a sense of divine timing than I did opening this book at this exact time. At every new paragraph, I was stopping and journaling or crying at what I was uncovering about myself. This book provided a week-by-week course filled with deep topics, an actionable framework, and the questions I desperately needed to crack myself open. The instances of serendipity that got this to me were now resonating.

In just the first three chapters, I hesitantly reclaimed a forgotten identity as a creative person. Always presenting as the practical one in the room over the course of my career, my identity had become synonymous with strategy more than creativity. I had unknowingly accepted it. Through the work in this book, I slowly remembered my love for writing and dance. While doing the exercises, two profound things happened. First, I found the very best tool I could ask for in this work—the morning pages. I'm obsessed with self-reflection, and morning pages have allowed me, in real time, to uncover thought patterns and fears that have been holding me back (more on this later).

Secondly, I learned that by eliminating creativity in my life, I'd been cutting off my own flow of energy, thus, keeping me stagnant and frustrated. I needed both an intake and an expression. When I started writing and dancing again, both things I already knew how to do, it took me through an incredible release of emotions I had been suppressing for some time.

I struggled with the idea of being a beginner again. Especially within creative expression. The world renders us so judgmental when people are brave enough to show up creatively. And that sucks. But I watch my kids be beginners all of the time, and I encourage them to believe the progress is what makes it fulfilling. Somewhere along the way, we grow up, and the world squeezes out the space for us to practice, forcing us to show up perfected. That is not where I want to be anymore, but it's hard. One of the things I had to face with this work is the persona of perfection that I'd been hiding under all along. The facade of having it all figured out was literally making me sick. And when I wasn't perfect, I'd opt out. Then, eventually, I gave up the things that made me who I am and turned into a shell of a person, pretending to do things that other people would find valuable. That's not a life.

I took these tasks seriously and challenged myself to find pockets of courage. I tried something new: painting. An ad online showed me a local watercolor class (the algorithm always comes through), so I signed up and went alone. I learned the basics of watercolor, sat with people just as insecure and curious about painting as I was, and enjoyed my progress through the three-hour class. I came home excited to be a beginner. Then, after ruminating about it in my journal for a few days, I got online and revamped an old blog. I had started writing several years ago, but eventually stopped, likely because of my own insecurities. Later that day, another friend texted me her new Substack. We chatted about her own journey, and I took it as another sign. I created a Substack too. It was important for me to push myself to be seen, and these platforms felt like a good first step.

Creative expression intertwined into my days had made a huge difference. It's this flow of energy that creates momentum and inspiration. Without this, the rest of the work I've done wouldn't have been possible. I find myself loosely touching creativity as it inspires me. I might read a post, be inspired to write something of my own, then get stuck on an idea, so I'll go and paint something for a little, and the meditative qualities of the painting clear my mind enough to unlock the words I was looking for. Then I might have a new idea to rearrange artwork in my home or swap pillows in different rooms. It may seem simple, but it's all flow.

I wrote on my iPad outside in the sunshine, watching the birds fly around my yard. I danced in my basement to music so loud it shook the house. I painted on my deck using a palette of only purple because it's my favorite color. I colored in a coloring book while watching my favorite show. I'd play with clay my kids had from when they were little when I was feeling bored of my other things. Creativity had given me permission to play. You can't be creative if you're not having fun.

While I was doing these things, I was also extremely embarrassed—even though I was literally home alone. I'd do stuff before the kids woke up or when they were at their dad's. I'd keep my supplies out of our main areas. The belief I had about productivity and how I spent my time was really crippling. I was embarrassed by the judgement of people who weren't even around. These voices of judgement were clearly just representing my own inner voice. I found so much joy in these exercises and had awoken a part of me that had been dormant for decades. I had let my inner child out—but only in secret. I still had a long way to go.

I highly recommend *The Artist's Way.* We are all inherently creative. This book has everything you need to tap into your own creative self.

| 5 |

Journaling

I didn't start journaling until my late thirties, at the recommendation of one of the self-help books I was devouring. I wrote in pencil—I wanted the option to erase my own thoughts. I didn't know myself at all and was afraid of what I'd see on those pages. Writing in pencil was like squinting at myself in the mirror, too afraid to fully open my eyes. I was terrified to put my thoughts out there, but determined to try something—anything—to get out of my own way. I reassured myself that I could always throw it away. But even the thought of those words existing outside of my head felt too risky. I gave myself an option to erase my own existence.

I'd write occasionally, usually during a sleepless night. I'd unload my discontentment about my relationship, drone on about frustrations at work, and tiptoe into my feelings about my parents. During the pandemic, I leaned into gratitude journaling. This was my first experience of actually being able to shift my mindset through a tangible action I had learned about. With practice, I became more consistent at writing down my experiences, and after I got divorced, my journal became my best friend. I was building foundational self-confidence and had discovered my own voice enough to write in pen. I had grown to a place where I could fill a drawer with completed journal inserts. I was no longer afraid of my own existence.

By the time my summer of transformation came around, I felt advanced as a journal writer. There's something about having to write the words down—to fully articulate the thought—that pushes me to the limit of my own feelings. And that's what it became for me: my book of feelings. Though limited (I had lived many decades thoroughly trying to avoid my feelings), this was the first time I no longer had to keep the ones I let through inside. I'd carry around my journal like a proud mama holding these newly born feelings. They were outside of my body, but I wasn't ready to let them get far.

Stream-of-consciousness journaling had proved valuable, but morning pages (as mentioned in the previous chapter from *The Artist's Way*) took it to a new level. Morning pages require the discipline of three full pages every day. It might not seem like a lot, but facing three blank pages, every single morning, forces you to push through that stopping point that your brain puts up to protect you. I noticed I was running out of stuff to say only about half way through. Pausing to acknowledge that I had addressed the most pressing items forced me to relax into my thoughts and take the time to confront the deeper, underlying feelings and beliefs I had become so skilled at ignoring. After some practice, I decided it was safe to dive a little deeper.

I love writing. It's the only way I can express the deepest parts of me, and I feel like I exist to share those depths. I'm moved by the tiniest moments—a glimpse of the mountains as the sun pours over them on my drive home from my kid's school, or the way my favorite cherry tree makes me feel enveloped in its embrace as I walk though my yard. I feel small moments deeply, and I want to capture that magic. I also crave deep meaning and symbolism and long for things to connect. I spend a lot of time diving deeply into events and actions because finding answers makes me feel safe.

To expand into the next version of myself, my journaling had to expand as well. I needed spaces to process different things differently. I wanted to ride the wave of momentum I found through synchronicities, and explore the depths of my own psyche. Both felt equally important.

Morning pages became a fundamental tool for my growth. Committing to daily, deep exploration quickly unearthed several underlying fears and beliefs I would need to address. The discipline of a morning routine also immediately impacted my mindset. In the first month, my pages were filled with gripes, irritants, and honestly, a lot of whining. I learned that, despite years of growth, the negative voice in my head was still too loud. My inner critic was incessant, and frankly, she was an asshole. I was stuck in a negative feedback loop I needed help breaking free from.

By the second month, I could sense a shift. I was starting to get a grip on my inner dialogue. I began recognizing patterns—fear and self-doubt disguised as excuses, over-analyzing, and playing the victim of others' actions. Reading my own words over and over allowed me to flush out harmful patterns of behavior and begin transitioning out of them. I noticed I was looking for excuses to skip the hard stuff. I also picked up on my dismissal of my needs. It was easier now that I was out of the situations that had brought me so much stress to see that I was addicted to the stress. Now, I was just creating it out of thin air. I had already done the seemingly hard thing—leaving the environments that held me back—but old habits (and belief systems) die hard. Once I had identified my repeated triggers, I saw my behavior loop clearly—right there on the page. The great thing about brains is that, once they recognize something as harmful, they can help you stop. I finally got out of my head and moved to the next step—identifying actual feelings.

Feelings took up most of month two. My learned coping mechanism from childhood was to fully disconnect my head and my body. Being in my head felt safer than acknowledging what my body was feeling. Eventually, I forgot most feelings altogether. I lived in numbness—which is useful in a crisis but a terrible way to live. Now, aware of my triggers and behavior, I had nowhere to go but into the sensations of those triggers.

I had no vocabulary of feelings beyond generic labels. I had even printed out an emotions wheel but couldn't connect the words to sensations beyond mad, sad, frustrated, or the absence of those. Everything felt like a tight knot in my chest. Journaling helped me identify new sensations: fear, betrayal, abandonment, horror, anger, grief, amusement, joy, peace, shame, gratitude, disgust, contentment, love. I researched and defined these words to match my body sensations, and eventually, I could match feelings to my actual physical experience. By writing about how I felt every day, I gradually recognized the chest knot as a call for attention. From there, the feeling would morph, usually bringing on a heavy stream of tears. Slowly, I taught myself how to acknowledge, understand, and truly feel my emotions.

This went on for most of the summer. Crying out layers of unprocessed grief and years of built-up terror from childhood almost became routine. (I dive into the depths of this processing more in a later chapter.) I asked myself if I would look back and call this time my "summer of feelings" or "my summer of tears." It sounds depressing, but honestly, it was freeing. Journaling had slowly tethered together the disconnection between my mind and my body—something I desperately needed so I could evolve. It was also—through this discipline—the tool that unlocked why I felt the way I did. The space on the pages left room to keep asking the questions necessary in understanding what would need to be addressed. You don't walk into something like this knowing where all your trauma lies—even after years of self-help and therapy. It's a process of discovery.

By the third month of morning pages, this process had almost fully transitioned my writing topics to gratitude, hope, ideas, and imagination. I had broken the pattern of self-sabotage and unlocked new tools for my future. And all from just writing down whatever was in my mind for three pages a day. This positive space allowed me to recognize feelings bubbling up before they became tight knots, and I could quickly identify the little gremlins of core wounds trying to show their heads. A quick acknowledgement, the attention to process, and a reframing of my truths, and I'd be on my way in minutes.

This disciplined journaling became a framework for rapid transformation. I graduated to joyful, colorful gel pens and two gorgeous notebooks gifted to me over the years by the same friend who had prompted me to pick up *The Artist's Way* in the first place. I love full-circle synchronicity.

As my thoughts expanded, so did my journaling tools. It was essential for me to keep morning pages sacred, so I opened new channels of expression.

Everything Journal: This journal became the home for all my random thoughts. I'd work out ideas for a new design aesthetic I was exploring or journal about a new meditation technique I was learning. Sometimes, I'd write stories to myself about my day or capture profound, deeply personal experiences I had with a partner. I used this journal to validate myself—I'd document successes and moments of triumph. I'd talk about a recipe I nailed or how I received an affirmation from someone that meant a lot to me. There are no rules for my everything journal; it's where all my shades are free to roam. My handwriting is often illegible, and I don't worry about grammar or spelling. I use whichever pen color I vibe with at the moment, and I even let myself draw pictures.

An unexpected outcome of this work was being able to build a strong muscle of self-validation. For a people-pleaser, this is huge. After a few weeks of sharing my good news with myself, in my journals, instead of seeking other people's opinions, I realized I preferred my own excitement over what I was getting from others. When something moved me, I'd immediately picture my journal—the brown faux leather cover with moon cycles on it—and feel fulfilled. I knew I'd go there and give myself the best advice or recognition as I penned the experience in the vivid purple ink of my favorite pen. It turns out, no one is a bigger fan of me than me!

I let go of holding onto all my feelings until I could align schedules with a girlfriend or emotionally dumping through text to that one person who held space for my randomness. I also stopped feeling disappointed if I didn't get the responses I was hoping for—whether in timing or enthusiasm. Suddenly, I had broken free from a cycle of external validation that had been perpetuating my negative belief that I was unlovable or not good enough.

This became a critical step in my healing and transformation. Shifting from external to internal validation helped me stay aligned with my true wants and needs—and honestly, it was really fun to celebrate literally everything with myself. I didn't have to justify that something was good enough to share to enjoy it. The little butterfly that flew near me, the new patch of grass I was growing in my yard, the fact that I kept a hanging plant alive during a hot, dry July. I got to celebrate all of it. Suddenly, my world became abundant with joy.

Visual Journaling: As my journaling expanded, I felt compelled to memorialize moments using words and imagery together—in a visual diary. I created a private Instagram account that serves as a timeline of my journey, allowing me to express myself more easily in the moment. Some posts are deep and vivid—like the one where exhaustion and loneliness felt all-encompassing, accompanied by an image of flowers in a meadow turning brown for the winter. Others are spontaneous—like the day the sunrise on my back porch moved me to tears of gratitude for the time I now have back in my life.

The account stays private, helping me resist the urge to write for others. While I rarely revisit my other journals, I love looking back at this platform to see how my images evolve alongside my personal growth. My page beautifully summarizes my story. Reflecting on those moments can be tough, but it always feels good to see how far I've come. Just imagine for a moment, what you might post on a platform if you knew no one would see it but you.

Curated Journal: Finally, I have a curated journal—a physical book adorned with beautiful watercolor butterflies and inspirational quotes throughout. I use it to write letters and lessons to myself and others. For example, I've written several letters to myself from the future in this book. I'll date the top of the page in the future, describe the amazing things happening in my life, express how I feel about them, and then leave it to the universe to guide me there.

The last time I did this, I was drawn to pick up the book on the exact day I had written the letter for. My routine had gotten randomly derailed one morning and I found myself on the floor in my bedroom at my vision boards, looking to swap out some images. I knew I had unused clippings in my dresser, and as I started going through drawers, I came across and picked up my butterfly journal and started flipping through it. I'd forgotten about it, but when I saw a date at the top of the page, I realized it was today's date! I'm obsessed with these synchronicities. I read the letter and was amazed at how true everything I had envisioned for myself a year ago had become. I floated through that day, knowing how proud my past-self would be of where I am now.

I also use this book to paste cutouts of quotes that resonate with me, writing reflections around them. I write letters to people who are no longer in my life and to those who are yet to enter. It's like a little book of both closure and manifesting.

I share all of this to show that journaling is one of the fundamental tools needed to uncover the personal insights essential for self-transformation. It can take on many forms, and there's an endless array of styles to suit your needs. The point is to fully articulate your feelings. You can't think yourself into transformation—you have to physically feel and move your way through it. The real lessons, the ones that catalyze big changes, are hidden just deep enough that you can only reach them with intentional precision. Writing is magic in this way.

| 6 |

The Posters

A few weeks into the summer, I felt like I had made a re-spectable amount of progress for my "time off." But with each passing day, the fear of what to do next still loomed. The good news was, I had cleared out enough mental junk to hear what felt like only my own thoughts now. However, my brain became an eruption of random and chaotic ideas, overwhelming me. The thing about walking away from the life you'd pigeonholed yourself into, is that having endless options can be immensely terrifying. I was still desperate for a guide for what comes next.

My instinct was to shut down. My nervous system was not safe enough to see opportunity, my belief systems hadn't been touched, and my confidence was very low. I was still very out of alignment. I needed a way to get it out and organize it. Maybe finding a sense of order would help me piece together this puzzle and find some direction.

How could I see into my own head? Even journaling some of these thoughts felt too chaotic. They came in small pieces, evolving every day as I learned something new. The tornado of ideas shifted constantly, making it hard to keep up. The undercurrent of fear about not having a "plan" was strong. I needed a working tool to calm the chaos and evolve with the rapid pace in my head.

One morning, I grabbed some old poster board left over from a school project, some sticky notes laying around, and just started scribbling. I had no idea what would come out or how it would help me; I just wanted to see it all spread out on a big poster to make sense of it. As the sticky notes began collecting, I immediately categorized them—facts about who I am, things I'm good at, things I desire. *Excellent, this is a self-discovery phase. I'm cracking open the dialogue about who I am versus who I have been existing as.* I carried the sticky notes around for days, jotting down observations like a biographer getting to know their subject.

After a few days, I realized how hard it was to "see" myself. Writing down observations and thoughts about who I really was—without curating them to fit some persona—felt awkward and cringey. This wasn't a professional bio, a summary for social media, or an interview. It was just me, in my own skin, trying to acknowledge what really made me, me—not some curated image I put together for other people to like. I couldn't edit out the parts I was embarrassed about; that would defeat the whole purpose. I also struggled with what was true. Were these things I had made up about myself?

It was clear that my self-worth was on trial. I had spent two years learning the basics of loving myself enough to leave everything that no longer fit, but this was deeper. This was a core wound that wouldn't be healed with new hobbies, self-care, and healthy boundaries. I wasn't sure what to do with that yet, so I just kept going with the sticky notes.

One of the notes uncovered my desire to become a published writer. The note appeared effortlessly on the board like it had been resurrected from an old life. When I looked at it, I felt a small ping in my gut—it was faintly familiar. This had been the first thing I read back to myself that had elicited any sort of emotion. I made a

note of the sensation and wondered if this was the feeling I should
be focused on.

From there, a flood of new ideas of what I could do started
to flow—speak, blog, coach, learn graphic design—I found myself
grabbing another color, and the notes evolved into ideas for who I
wanted to become and what I wanted to do. *Perfect, some direction.* I
kept repeating the exercise—make notes, walk away, revisit them,
keep what still resonated, remove what didn't, add new ideas.

This brainstorming process unfolded over about three weeks.
Each day, I'd pick up my poster, and half of the board felt like
it held someone else's ideas. Allowing myself to explore every
thought—knowing I could discard them the next day if they didn't
fit—became both liberating and essential. I realized that I needed
the random ideas to uncover the ones that created a spark. And
also that what caused a spark one day, might feel like a full-body
"no" the next.

This creative process was provoking my perfectionism. I was
still plagued by the insecurity that someone else might judge what
I put on there.

Teach a dance class—er, no, take a dance class—er, no, choreo-
graph a dance—no, er, study choreography.

Create a website—no, er, write a blog—er, no, write a
book—no, er, read a book about writing—no, take a writing class.

My mind played tricks on me and, my inner critic was relent-
less, with thoughts like, "That won't make you any money," or
"You're too old," or "You don't have credentials," swirling around.
Eventually, I grew annoyed enough with her that I made a con-
scious effort to silence her, and everything went on the board.
She's mean.

I remember my mom telling me stories about how her options were teacher, nurse, or secretary. I remember thinking that the fifteen options I had were amazing compared to three. Now, there are too many options to count. The rule book has been burned, but the limiting beliefs are still in there.

When I powered through my insecurities enough to give in to the intent of the exercise, the internal struggle revealed an important perspective: there is always going to be someone smarter, better, faster, more experienced, more talented, more whatever than you. That is irrelevant. You are all of those things to someone else. I've heard this before, and understood it, but until I was faced with creating a path of my own choices, I didn't fully feel it.

I thought about the things I was consuming. Almost every person on a podcast, on TV, in the ads I'm served is now younger than me. I'm listening to advice on podcasts from people who have been doing things for five years...five years! I have done a million things for five years. I could have one-hundred "expert" podcasts by now. All of this is made up. The new rules are, dig past the noise in your head, find out what you like to do, and just go do it. Someone wants what you have.

Eventually, I curated three posters with six total sections (detailed below). I now had a directional guide full of my own thoughts and ideas. The solitude and consistency of this exercise helped me weed out other people's expectations and opinions on who I was and what I could do. These posters captured all the thoughts spinning in my head. They were a visual representation of my own voice staring back at me—and hidden inside were the questions and answers for how I'd get to the other side.

My Final Poster Outline:

Poster I
Side A. Self-discovery and observation: Every time I noticed something about myself, realized a truth, or discovered an insight or philosophy.
Side B. *The Artist's Way*: Every task went on here—completed and to do.

Poster 2
Side A. My abundance list: How I wanted to feel every day to live my best, highest, and most aligned life.
Side B. Abundance practices: Mantras, actions, and beliefs that made the abundance list true.

Poster 3
Side A. Purpose-aligned projects: Things I felt called to do, separate from outcomes or monetization. These had no expectation or assumption of outcome.
Side B. Income generating ideas: Things that aligned with my abundance list and could potentially be a new career direction.

Poster 1A. I needed a way to learn who I was. These notes started extremely simply. I put things down like "I love green tea." "I am a ballet dancer." " I am a fast learner." "I believe being a good parent means showing up, all the time." You get the point. I needed to find the things that made me, me, and then learn them from an outside perspective. (I go deeper into this in the "Main Character Energy" chapter.)

Poster 1B. Fresh out of two decades of corporate America, I was still deeply addicted to productivity. No longer going back and forth to a job, I still felt obligated to justify how I spent my time. To whom, though? Me? Onlookers? My retired neighbors? This need for validation was a crutch, but I recognized it as part of weaning myself off the toxic productivity mindset. Tracking my accomplishments helped me satisfy that urge until I learned to let it go; it also gave me something to rattle off to friends and family. The notes here listed the books I'd read, classes I'd taken, projects I'd tackled—everything that had filled my days since I left my job.

However, while I once needed this structure to track my progress, I've grown into someone who believes the most important opinion is mine. Now, simply existing feels like enough. Today, the only note I'd need on this board would say, "I exist, and that is enough."

Poster 2A. My abundance list. Abundance is a paradox—we are all inherently abundant. The question is: what are you abundant in? I realized I had many things that I was abundant in that I loved, but there were some that weren't aligned with what I truly wanted. I needed to curate this abundance intentionally and identify actionable steps to shift toward what mattered.

For example, before I quit my job, I was constantly frustrated by a lack of time. My days were packed with work, a long commute, and commitments I didn't truly want. I decided that time was one of my most valuable resources, so I put that at the top of my list: "I am abundant in time." Now, I know not everyone has the option of just quitting, but there are ways to begin negotiating your time to move it up on your own scale. (We'll cover that in 2B.)

This part is all about defining your ideal abundance list. Mine includes "Self-Worth, Health, Ease, Love, Creativity, Financial Freedom." Initially, the list had about twelve items, which I carefully whittled down to six. Part B of this board will help you assess if you're truly committed to achieving these priorities.

Poster 2B. Now that my list felt right, it was time to reframe. I found that this ended up being a collection of beliefs, mantras, and actions. For each item, I asked, "What would make this true?" and from there, created a new list. I used the same disciplined process as before: add things, walk away, revisit, edit. Every morning, I pulled out this poster and read it aloud until I believed it. Within days, I could feel my attitude changing.

I found that when I became comfortable in this exercise of daily abundance affirmations, I'd have to acknowledge that there were stickies on there that I didn't fully believe in. For example, in my health section, I'd written an action for myself to do eight thousand steps a day—a number that was unrealistic given the work I had set out to do that summer. Each day, I felt a pang of failure and shame as I saw it, knowing I wasn't meeting it, nor was I going to. Eventually, I just took it off and replaced it with something attainable that aligned with my abundance of health: "Movement every day—walk, yoga, dance, weights." This shift allowed me to believe in it, feel fulfilled, and as a result, I naturally increased my walking.

This is *not* a goals list. It's an abundance list. The things on here just needed to affirm how I was *already* abundant in these areas. This became foundational for shifting my belief system.

Poster 3A. This poster became the place to calm my overwhelm of endless opportunities. It started from the idea of becoming a published author, and then I evolved it into exploring the things I would do if earning money wasn't a constraint. This was my "If I won the lottery today, what would I do?" list. Throughout my life, I have been conditioned out of play, so this list needed to be fun and whimsical and creative. It had book writing on it, but it also had "become a tattooed ballerina fairy." I didn't want to lose the permission to play in my life. If I had just created a potential job list, I'd surely have found myself right back in the creatively stifled, overworking, energy-sucking world of productivity as a form of value. That could no longer be an option.

Poster 3B. The practical poster. This was the one to quiet the nagging voice reminding me that my financial independence was temporary. I brainstormed everything I had the skills to do, along with the things I was interested in and could be educated or trained for. From there, I connected these ideas to my abundance list. Would pursuing another senior executive job conflict with my desire for an abundance of time? Yes. Did it align with my newly discovered beliefs about myself? No. Did it meet my budget requirements? Yes. Was I willing to give up my self-discovery and my time for money? No. And so on. This board challenged me to rethink society's expectations and my own, pushing me to consider traditional notions of trading time for money. I sat there for days wishing I had done this exercise in my apartment back in college, before making major life decisions.

I kept this separate from 3A because the quote, "Love what you do, and you'll never work a day in your life," sets an impossible standard. There's freedom in having activities that aren't tied to specific outcomes—and I believe there's room for both in a fulfilling life. I also believe in building a lifestyle that truly aligns with who I am. I've tried the "grin and bear it" approach, sprinting up the ladder, letting that one part consume everything, hoping for relief at the top. That's a ruse.

The posters did exactly what I needed—they took the incessant swirling ideas from my mind and put them into something tangible, something I could actually work with. The creative process of deciding what stayed on the boards and what didn't felt like a cathartic "choose your own adventure," mapping out what my life could potentially be. It made me reflect on my true nature, dig deep to uncover hidden desires, and face my insecurities. Most great projects start with brainstorming, so why should my life be any different?

The posters allowed me to breathe a huge sigh of relief. I didn't have all the answers or a clear path forward, but I had a direction and what felt like the right questions to guide me. Knowing that misalignment had been the catalyst for blowing up my life meant that rebuilding it would require addressing those wrong turns. Now, my mind could finally calm down—I had a place to put everything it had been screaming at me to pursue. From here, my appetite for real change would be tested, as I set out to confront everything standing between me and the life I'd organized on these posters. With that direction, the real work began.

| 7 |

New Habits

I felt the momentum. My energy had shifted. The rediscovery of myself as a creative had been astounding. The uncovering of my truths continued as I worked iteratively on my posters. I was feeling new in a lot of ways. Tapping into creativity and play gave me purpose, and this energy helped me to chart a direction. I was optimistic that I had uncovered a path to a new life.

As I worked through the abundance list on my posters, I knew the next step was to implement new, aligned habits. I started with movement. It might seem obvious, but I hadn't realized how crucial movement would be in healing the deep wounds I needed to face. I had read about somatic therapy and tried a few exercises I found online, but it wasn't until I started dancing again that I remembered how connected movement, energy, and expression are.

Shifting my mindset to movement for expression, rather than exercise, was essential. Exercise always felt forceful and regimented. I struggled to stick with it because it didn't align with my mood or what my body craved. Finally, I let go of the rules and decided to follow what my body told me—not some program designed without me at its center.

I picked movement types I didn't dread: ballet, walking, yoga, stretching, and free weights. All activities I enjoyed—when in the mood. Structure and redundancy didn't suit me, which is funny since ballet, my foundation, is one of the most disciplined dance styles. I guess years of pink tights, black leotards, and rigid rules had me yearning for rebellion. There was something amazingly freeing about doing barre at home with my tattoos showing, messy hair, and whatever athleisure I felt like wearing that day.

Dancing brought back the ability to feel emotions through my body. The energy surge that comes when movement and music collide is magical. I let go of the rules and let my body roam. On low-energy days—physical or mental—I chose walking or weights. The freedom to choose my movement each day was what finally clicked for me.

Through these new habits, I had come a long way in expressing myself. The posters helped me get out of my head, journaling kept me out of my head, and movement released emotions from my body. I now had space to fill myself back up. Some days I bubbled with ideas and expression; other days, I felt depleted and craved balance. I realized I needed both—expression and nourishment.

Mentally, I needed to be fed. I like to think of feeding my brain on a sliding scale. One end is mindless, silly, and "unproductive." The other end is deep, intellectual, and educational. I enjoy the entire spectrum—it reminds me to make space for fun. What worked best for me was a variety of books. Some were fun, easy reads with interesting characters and drama. Others were deep, resonant stories, like memoirs of people overcoming trauma or dealing with complex PTSD. I also gravitated toward educational books on topics that intrigued me—often recommended by friends or served to me by the algorithm.

Podcasts and media sometimes filled the gaps, but I prefer things that don't always require a screen. Self-help books that resonate with me, or instructional books on specific skills, also fit in.

For example, I read a book on how to meditate because I like to understand fundamentals before diving in.

What changed was curating my intake list to align with my abundance list. Every book I chose was connected to something I was shifting toward—whether it was ease, play, self-worth, or creativity. Nothing was random anymore. If it had a place in my life, it needed to align with the life I wanted.

The most important part about what I was deciding to take on was how it was making me feel. Was the information I was consuming making me feel the emotions I wanted to feel more of? That was the big test. My emotions (literally energy in motion) were creating my reality. So, if I wasn't thinking and creating my own emotions, was I responding to my outside environment appropriately for my new life?

Making big changes to my life had given me the insight into what it means to leave a situation that isn't working for you anymore. It frees up so much space for what you actually want. But was I then filling this space with things that mimicked those old feelings? What were my choices about media telling me I needed to pay attention to? I had more control over my life than I thought.

Then, I decided to tackle an old foe: meditation. I had tried it many times, downloaded apps, taken friends' advice, and attended group classes. Nothing had worked. My mind raced, or I'd fall asleep from sheer exhaustion. Meditation always felt premature.

But now, with my habits and beliefs evolving, I felt a nudge to try again. I had been exploring Joe Dispenza's work as well as the law of attraction, and with enough understanding of the science behind brain changes, I was ready to use meditation for something beyond "mindfulness."

I tried another guided meditation, and this time, I was pleasantly surprised. The thoughts that used to race through my mind were no longer there—thanks to morning pages and movement.

Plus, I was well-rested and no longer over-scheduled. I could finally feel the full benefits of this practice. Meditation quickly became one of the most impactful things I added to my life.

I made meditation the first thing I did each morning—before to-do lists, dream analysis, or any limiting beliefs could creep in. Guided meditations from YouTube creators I connected with set the perfect tone (hello, deep voice with an Australian accent). There's science behind how brainwaves work during sleep transitions and the influence between the conscious and unconscious mind. At a minimum, starting my day with a guided morning meditation flooding my mind with positivity changed how the rest of my day unfolded. It's been a game-changer for me.

Just like with my other habits, I threw out the rule book. I meditate lying down in bed. I don't overthink my posture or temperature—I just focus on intention. So who cares how I'm positioned? And if you need headphones or have to adjust your routine because of life, that's fine. Try things out. Within days, I genuinely felt like a different, happier, more fulfilled person.

In adjusting my days to include these new habits, I realized something big. Yes, this was about habits, but it highlighted that my focus would ultimately dictate my life. The intentional choices I was making to implement these habits were leading me directly into present-moment awareness. Suddenly, my days were filled with moments where I had to stop and make a conscious decision about what to do next. I had asked for time and choices, and now I was living them.

Since I refused to set a strict schedule or force myself into a routine, I had to stay in the moment to know what I truly wanted. Then it hit me—the reason I'd been resisting routine was that it turned these habits into automation. I didn't want automation. That was a tactic I had used when burdened with too much to fit into my schedule. That had been my coping mechanism when I was overloaded, trying to squeeze too much into my schedule. It was a life of burnout, where productivity and box-checking gave me quick dopamine hits. But that approach bypassed the experience of actually living. Rejecting routine was helping me lift my head up and stop powering through life. Staying aware of my actions, all the time, allowed me to stay connected to my intuition. I knew my new life wasn't going to be filled with mindless activities set on a schedule. I wanted to truly feel my way through life, to actually live it. Without a schedule, I began shifting my awareness out of the future and the past and into the present. This was an awakening.

PART 3

| 8 |

Main Character Energy

My lack of identity had been staring me down for some time. Figuring out that I had this issue was easy—finding out who I was, not so much. I'd recognized, and had even leveraged, how good I had become at reading other people. My most recent position at work had been built around it. This made it all the more frustrating to not know myself. It was a survival tactic I had mastered—knowing others showed me who I should be around them. But when I turned the mirror inward, all I saw was nothingness. I existed only to reflect others back to themselves.

In the two years after my divorce, I felt completely exposed. Withdrawing from my ex's life—his family, hobbies, friends—left me painfully aware of my lack of identity. I had few remaining friendships, no hobbies or passions, and barely any family to support me. What I did have was tied up in my roles as a professional and a mom—two identities already hard enough to balance.

I never felt important enough to have my own identity. Childhood trauma and my abandonment wounds destined me to be the supporting character in other people's lives. But I knew that had to change. First, I had to convince myself that I was the main character in my own life. Leaving my marriage and my job helped strip away the noise. Suddenly, I was left with a void to fill, and it became clear I had a lot of work ahead.

I tried to piece together a timeline of my life that was about me—accomplishments and memories that weren't tied to my mom's cancer or my ex. It was a pitiful exercise at first, but I scraped together some milestones: accolades, projects, jobs, births. It gave me a starting point.

Next, I pulled out all of my old photo albums. I organized the pictures in chronological order, looking to curate a new narrative about my past. With each photo I placed, I studied it, placed myself back in the scene, and tried to remember the moments surrounding that image. What were my feelings? What did I care about? I focused on making myself the main character and paid attention to the story I was living. It helped, but I yearned for a tool that was more concrete.

I revisited my Enneagram (Type 3) results, which I had taken during couples counseling. I remember reading those results during counseling and feeling like someone had observed my life with a microscope. I wrote down some insights that stood out. Then I turned to astrology—Virgo sun, Libra rising, Scorpio moon—hoping the stars would offer the insight I couldn't find elsewhere. I wanted something that resonated beyond the obvious.

Using these tools, I put together a worksheet to understand myself better. *What excites me? What matters to me? What am I good at? What drives me?* I stared at those blank sections, initially paralyzed, then slowly filling them in with what I had gathered from my Enneagram and astrology chart.

What excites me?
- In-depth study, and transformative experiences.
- Showing up for the underdog
- Deep connections and sharing knowledge
- Creating rituals of healing and comfort

- Creating specific aesthetics

It was just words copied from these third-party descriptions of me, but it felt true. I studied this list often, tucking it into the front of my journal. The exercise validated how misaligned my old life had been. The words I wrote described someone completely different from who I had been. There was no way I could have integrated these parts of me into my old life. I felt relief, knowing I was on the back end of walking away from that.

This was the foundation I needed to build a life that was mine, not one where I risked losing myself. I committed to letting the rest unfold as it needed to.

Then, during a conversation with a friend, she listened and offered advice, something I usually craved. But this time, something clicked. I told her, "Just because I *can* do it doesn't mean I *want* to." As soon as I said it, I felt a shift. It had only been a few weeks since I was desperate for someone to tell me what I should do. I had spent years proving I could do anything thrown at me, but now, I wasn't looking for approval anymore. There was finally a crack in the walls surrounding who I truly was. That tiny opening—exposing glimpses of my authentic self—was a promise of freedom and an invitation to keep chipping away. That was the journey I would continue.

Before we hung up, she threw me another suggestion: "Have you ever looked into human design?" I hadn't, but I wrote it down. She's one of those friends who always gives me nudges that turn out to be profound, so I paid attention. Then as soon as we hung up, I did a deep dive.

Reading my human design—my energy type, authority, profile, strategy—was revelatory. It felt as though I'd been gifted a user manual for my soul. These descriptions brought a profound recognition and acknowledgement of who I truly was. There, written out as explanations and gifts, were qualities I'd pushed away, hidden, or ignored to either "fit in" or "be successful." It was like the final piece of a long-unsolved puzzle clicking perfectly into place—a feeling of everything aligning in one fluid, undeniable moment. There's a satisfying, almost magical sensation when you realize that all the scattered fragments of yourself, the parts you've wrestled with or tucked away, suddenly connect. It's as if an invisible mechanism within you locks into alignment, and you can feel the gentle release of tension you hadn't fully realized you were holding. In that moment, I felt like I could stop searching and piecing things together. It was an overwhelming relief that said, "Yes, this is exactly who I am."

Two important truths stood out. First, I didn't need to finish everything I started. (Wait, what?) Coming from a world of deadlines and project launches, this blew my mind. I'm an ideas person—I love learning and strategizing, but once I've gotten what I need, I'm ready to move on. I'm a "you're done when you finish what's on your plate" kid. I'd also struggled with feeling compelled to move on from connections (mostly at work) after I'd learned what I needed from that person. It felt selfish and opportunistic. My ex had shamed me for moving on to new hobbies too quickly, claiming I'd tire of the next one in a few months, so why bother? He used it as an excuse to dismiss things I was excited about, making me feel like there was something wrong with me. But now, I had permission to rebel against those barriers and embrace this side of myself.

Second, I learned I was meant to respond to what comes to me, rather than forcing things to happen. Everything I needed would come through the people I knew, and this resonated deeply. Every time I'd pushed for something based on some rule book or external advice, rather than my intuition, it had led me down the wrong path. Letting go and trusting my intuition brought a profound sense of freedom from the limiting beliefs that had held me back.

These revelations gave me permission to be who I had always been. With these insights, I could confidently assess what was for me and what wasn't. Networking? No. Selling myself? No. Creative expression? Yes. Following my random trails of curiosity? Absolutely. From here, I updated Poster 3B, and I was thrilled to be on this new, aligned path.

I realized that everyone I had been performing for didn't know the real me. They only knew a version of me—one shaped by their own beliefs. It was all about perspective. I already knew no one cared more about me than I did, but now I saw how much energy I had wasted on worrying about others' opinions.

Here I was, having lived a full life, with potentially another full one ahead—this time with no societal road map. I had pieced together who I really was and built the confidence to do whatever the hell I wanted.

Reflecting on my old fears of aloneness, I realized that acknowledging my lack of support system had revealed something unexpected: freedom. There's an upside to being alone. I didn't have the burden of shifting family dynamics or the opinions of relatives. I wasn't responsible for parenting my parents or negotiating family holidays. I was free to do whatever I wanted—answering only to myself. As for my children, I would be the best parent I could, but beyond that, I was exempt.

From here, I crafted a new belief system to support my main-character energy. It had nothing to do with the lives of the people I knew, what anyone else was doing, or what I was "supposed" to do. My life was uniquely mine to live, and not living up to my full potential was a disservice to the greater good. I let go of the belief that suffering was required for success. The secret to life was joy—my joy.

My purpose now was to follow what aligned with me and sparked excitement. Finally, as the main character in my own life, I'd see each day as a reflection—everything now served as information about my inner world. Had I shifted my beliefs? Was I reflecting things that tested me? Was I reflecting things that supported me? Were coincidences and synchronicities cheering me on? Was contrast appearing as a sign to refocus my energy? I decided to take control. Everything was now working for me. I was the creator, with the road map in hand and fully in charge.

This new perspective gave me the confidence to rewrite other characters in my story—an antagonist (or even a villain), a side-kick, a confidant, a mentor, secondary characters, etc. Through this lens, I could reframe the people who had come in and out of my life and reconsider my feelings about them. No longer was I seeking attention or validation from people who were sometimes no longer even around, yet whose wounds still lingered. Now, I could ask myself what I had learned or was meant to learn from them.

This perspective led me to a new understanding of forgiveness. I've never been able to reconcile the idea of forgiveness; I blame the "distraught by injustice" part of my astrology chart. I get the whole "you take the poison and hope the other person dies" metaphor, but I'd always struggled to see forgiveness as a real path forward. Forgiveness often feels like absolving blame or erasing the act that caused harm—something my need for justice couldn't fully accept. But I also wanted to let some things go.

However, I could get behind the idea of character arcs—reframing actions as plot points in my story. Viewing someone as an antagonist in my life who helped me evolve or exposed the depth of my core wounds felt like the freedom I'd been seeking. Was this person an asshole? In that moment, absolutely (I believe that no one is all good or all bad). Did they show me how deeply I actually disliked myself? Absolutely. *So, thank you. Go on being an asshole, or don't, I really don't care.*

This approach let me reconcile that actions could be harmful, but I could still move on. It didn't dismiss pain that I'd given or received, but it allowed me to release any resentment I'd been holding. I didn't need to absolve anyone for their actions, and I accepted responsibility for my own. But now, I saw these experiences as part of my growth. This perspective kept the experience, shifted the narrative around it, and let me move on.

This was important closure. I had a lot of trauma to move through.

| 9 |

Envisioning the Future

With self-discovery solidly underway, I finally had the confidence to craft a better future for myself. Before, these exercises felt too foreign, as if I was designing a life for someone else. I had been good at that. But as I shed the coping mechanisms that had dominated my decisions, I felt safe imagining a life focused solely on me.

I started by adding a new vision board to the two I had created previously. Over time, I've swapped a few pictures as I evolved, but the boards still resonate. They live in my bedroom, where I see them every day. The images bring me joy, like a shrine to the life I'm building.

However, despite their beauty, these vision boards lacked something vital. I had always focused on what I wanted and how I would get it. But that tactic limited me to what I'd been exposed to. This next chapter was about expanding outside of the things shown in magazines and other media. At this time, I was studying the law of attraction—which throws out the ideas of "how and what" and forces you to focus on how you want to *feel*. That was it! How could I create a life I truly wanted without knowing how I wanted to feel? I realized that while goal-setting and reverse-engineering were skills I had mastered, they were also the very things holding me back.

To break free, I crafted an entire "ideal day." This was challenging because I had become so used to reacting to others that I lost the muscle for dreaming for myself. I started with a bullet point list in my notes app, pretending like I was independently wealthy. My list began with simple desires like "no alarm," "morning stretching," and "meeting a friend for lunch." It was basic but felt like a start.

A few months into the summer, I looked at the list and realized I was already living most of it. That was amazing, but it left me asking, "Now what?" The days were better, but I didn't want to settle for "better than awful." I wanted to elevate my life further, but I was stuck. Unlike those who know exactly what they want, I struggled to find clear examples of the life I desired. No one around me was living what I envisioned, and I found no media representation that made me say, "Yes, that's it!"

I searched for inspiration but came up short. So, I turned to Chat GPT. I typed a short journal entry based on my bullet list, included some sentences pulled from my character description paper, and then asked it to craft a story about my ideal day. The result? The bones of my new life. When reading it, about 80 percent of it lit me up. From there, I made edits until every word felt like the best version of me. I even gained new inspiration.

For example, where I had simply written "no alarm," ChatGPT wrote: "I wake up naturally, just as the first light of dawn filters through the large windows in my bedroom. The room is calm, filled with warm and cozy earth tones. The gentle scent of lavender lingers in the air. I take a moment to breathe in the peaceful silence, feeling a deep sense of gratitude." Blow me away—I live in a literal fairy tale.

I really latched onto the idea of feelings being the guide. However, I had just learned to feel feelings like a week ago, so it felt a little like being sent from kindergarten directly to college. Instead of job titles, income goals, or an itinerary of my day, I focused on feelings: free, inspired, comfortable, beautiful, in flow, safe, and abundant. Suddenly, the possibilities expanded, and I stopped limiting myself.

In my old life, I found "success" by controlling every detail, creating a false sense of safety. It worked, but it also burned me out and limited my growth. Letting go of details and relaxing into feelings was like floating in the sky and landing in a warm, soft, golden net of comfort—far better than the cold, heavy burden of certainty. Committing to this focus on feelings set me free.

When I felt forced to blow up my life, it was the frustration and trapped feelings that drove my need for freedom. My life had shrunk into a box of achieved goals, but inside, I felt empty because I never considered how I felt. By avoiding my emotions, I ended up trapped, dodging the same old tormentors of loss and abandonment. Where your focus goes, your life follows.

I applied this new learning by rewriting my narrative. Instead of saying, "I'm successful at my operational executive job where I work from home," I asked myself what I truly wanted. Did I really want success as defined by someone else? No, I wanted to feel fulfilled. An operational executive job wasn't the goal—it was too limiting. I didn't care what job I had, as long as it let me feel fulfilled. I also realized that working from home was just a means to feel freedom over my time. I wanted to live slowly, intentionally, and with purpose. I wanted to feel freedom and an abundance of choice. So, that might not actually be work from home. That could be project work or contract work. I didn't actually know all of the possibilities. So, I revised it to: "Financial freedom gives me the gift of time—time to live slowly, intentionally, and with purpose.

The success of my career is deeply fulfilling." By swapping specifics for feelings, my heart opened. The world became full of endless possibilities. I no longer needed to control every detail.

Once I fell in love with every word of my ideal day, I pinned it in my notes app. It became a tool to test my focus—was I focused on what I desired or what I feared? After years of focusing on what I didn't want, retraining my brain to focus on my desires took effort.

I went back to the idea that my life was my mirror. Feelings are guides, contrast is a guide, roadblocks are a guide. So are gratitude, excitement, and synchronicities. Each day became full of signs showing me what belonged in my life and what didn't.

This exercise not only evolved my writing, but it also helped me anchor in the present moment. To align with my ideal day, I had to consistently check in with my feelings, which required staying present. I quickly realized why the "present moment" has so much self-help space dedicated to it. We're often stuck in the past or fearing the future, but the present is the only real thing.

This was a significant realization. As someone who grew up surrounded by the trauma of a terminally ill mother, I had become bound by past trauma and had learned to fear the future and dismiss the present. But now, I was discovering that the present is all that exists. I had wasted so much time sacrificing the now because the future was so uncertain. And I had let the past rule everything as a way to try and correct it. But the truth is, I'll never be in the future or the past—I'll only ever be in the present.

Crafting my ideal day based on feelings, seeing my life as a mirror giving me clues all the time, and staying grounded in the present have fundamentally shifted my approach to everything. These tools have transformed my experience rapidly, allowing me to live in alignment with the life I've always wanted.

| 10 |

The Fundamental Shift

I had done the basics. I'd spent a decade reading self-help books. I was experienced in journaling and extremely self-aware. I was a master at observing other people, identifying who they were, and guiding them toward transformation. I'd even gone to therapy, twice. And don't get me wrong—I'd picked up a tremendous amount of learning along the way. That's why I'm even here. But there was a level I hadn't yet reached, a place deep down that I knew I'd have to go to if I wanted to get unstuck.

Both of my experiences in therapy were helpful, one more so than the other. My first therapist, a sweet and gentle woman who I found through my insurance, sat comfortably hugged in her cardigan across the room from me every two weeks. She prompted me gently with questions about how I felt about my life, what feelings I was experiencing, and encouraged me to seek appropriate support groups. She had no idea the thickness of the walls she would never penetrate, or the decades of polished performance she was up against. I enjoyed going because it forced me to articulate the things that were top of mind, and it ended up being the practice I needed for my transformational journaling that would come.

One session, a few months in, she paused during her questions. My throat closed in fear. Had she somehow seen through my facade? I desperately wanted her to, but was still terrified at the thought. She spoke deliberately: "You know, Lauren, you're an extraordinary woman. You went through a lot at a young age and have made a beautiful life for yourself." I winced, trying to hold back tears, partly because I didn't know how to accept praise, and partly because I was devastated that she hadn't seen through my performance. I never went back.

Years later, after the divorce, I went back to the therapist that I had seen through couples counseling. Those sessions had been successful in calmly and without drama dismantling a twenty-four-year, toxically intertwined, nostalgia-heavy, co-dependent relationship, and I desperately wanted someone with context about my situation. I was older and less worried about what other people thought of me than I was with my first therapist, so I knew she had already seen through my walls. She patiently tolerated my stubborn intellectualizing of my feelings, and recognized my desire for a sounding board to process my own thoughts. She was excellent at holding space for me, affirming my decisions, and letting me uncover my own revelations. She injected just enough of her own observation that it didn't leave me feeling too exposed.

She nudged, suggested, and guided without pressure, and then, at the exact right moment, she'd swoop in with a hit-you-in-between-the-eyes truth bomb. First, developmental trauma—a term I could deep dive into and acknowledge as something that had happened to me instead of something I was. There were actual consequences to living with someone who had a terminal illness. This was an answer I had been looking for.

Second, an observation: "What you experienced when you were younger with your mom being your sole caregiver and then dying, even though you were legally an adult, can be equated to someone who had been orphaned." This statement brought the weight and substance to my experience that I hadn't let come through before. Being orphaned was a big idea, and I immediately connected to the sense of feeling lost and alone that I had fought so hard against. Another profound statement of permission to acknowledge what I had been through and understand why I felt and behaved the way that I did.

Like I said, I had gotten a lot through therapy, but at this moment, I knew my patience and my bank account wouldn't withstand another go. Waiting a few weeks between sessions, spending time getting the therapist up to speed, and limiting the work to an hour-long appointment—it wasn't enough to spark the transformation I was seeking. I was past needing valuable insights and tools. I wanted something deeper. I needed someone to crack me open and dig up the unprocessed grief, the complex trauma, the repressed pain. I needed an excavation.

Even this summer, I'd gotten back to the basics. I'd organized my thoughts, implemented new habits, and found a tremendous sense of peace and optimism. I had evolved, sure, but I still hadn't transformed. I'd look at my posters and marvel at my glimmering new direction. I'd pat myself on the back for my new habits and mindset. I was swimming in gratitude, but I couldn't step into my gorgeous future because—I didn't truly believe I was her. I could play the part, but deep down, I didn't deserve that new main character life.

The stakes were too high to stop now. I had walked away from everything I had worked for. Every ounce of me knew that was still the right decision, but to go any further knowing I'd just be building another version of that old life—even if it felt shiny and new for a little—would eventually lead me right back here—facing my own beliefs.

I once told a friend that when I finally made it into the most exclusive meetings, the closed-door strategy sessions, and the top-tier decision-making rooms in my career, the imposter syndrome eventually melted away. I realized I brought more to the table than most people in those rooms. But there were two things they had that I didn't—money and audacity. And that was it—when you believe you're unworthy—even if it's way deep inside—you'll never truly live life the way you want to live it. I needed to heal to walk through life with the audacity to believe I deserved whatever I wanted.

I thought about going on a retreat or searching for a specific kind of therapist, but those ideas still felt like they wouldn't fully heal me. Eventually, I realized that the deep, dark places within me had only one person who could face them—me. And I'd have to do it by confronting what I'd been avoiding all along: I'd have to face it alone.

That word, *alone*, had always meant *abandoned, unwanted, left behind* to me. I had spent my life sprinting into other people's lives, seeking what felt like safe spaces to hide. Developing co-dependencies and adapting myself to fit into these foreign environments had been my way of coping. I'd become proficient at finding experts with answers—people I could pay to give me their knowledge, assessments, or insights. I was as terrified of being alone and listening to my own thoughts, as I had been of waiting for my mom to die. But in sacrificing my identity to avoid being alone, I'd done the worst thing I could—I had abandoned *myself*.

To truly heal, I had to give all that up (I was already far down that road), but I also had to resist the urge to run and hide in someone or something else again. I had the tools, the ability, and the time I needed. It was time to face myself—I just had to be brave.

MEMORY REVISION

The work I had been doing had given me the answers to the first test. My core wounds—the beliefs driving all my sabotaging behaviors—were my lack of self-worth and my nervous system constantly telling me I wasn't safe. I knew exactly where they came from. The abandonment issues from my parents' divorce at age eight, the death of my mom when I was nineteen, and the developmental trauma from the ten years leading up to her death watching her battle cancer. There were other, more run-of-the-mill traumas in there, but these were the main ones. My readings on complex PTSD and the day my second therapist equated my experiences to being orphaned had been light-bulb moments.

What I didn't know was, how to set myself free from a life sentence of emotional sabotage. I had tried EMDR therapy, which had helped me understand I had unprocessed feelings, but it hadn't changed how I felt about myself in the present.

I was missing large chunks of memories from my youth. I realized that to move forward as a whole person, I'd have to go back and meet the versions of me I couldn't remember. The self-discovery exercises I'd been doing confirmed this—many prompts asked me to recall what I used to love as a child. But I didn't remember any of that. Scraping through old photos and stories I'd been told just to find something authentic had been difficult.

Since journaling had been going well, I decided it would be my tool. I had a handful of memories to work with, so I chose one and wrote about it as if I were telling a story to someone else. I only got five sentences in before I broke down in full-body sobs. I had never gone back into those scenes before. I had only acknowledged the memories as facts—rehearsed, disassociated statements about a traumatic time. They were missing context, sensory details, and emotion. This was the dam about to break.

That first memory started a month of intense journaling, where I slowly and intentionally allowed myself the safety to revisit the life I had lived while my mom battled breast cancer and eventually died. I revisited the night she found a new lump on her head and made me touch it, the months she spent in the hospital after an experimental procedure almost killed her, the time she collapsed in the grocery store in front of a friend from school. I wrote about the last time I saw her and how I chose not to be there when she died, the phone call informing me of her death, the funeral planning cast solely on my shoulders at nineteen, the responsibility of closing her estate, and the inadvertent dismantling of my own life after she died. I processed twenty-year-old grief, uncovered moments of physical, emotional, and financial abandonment, and filled in major gaps in my memories.

Had it not been for years of prior healing work, I doubt I would have felt safe enough to go this deep. But with each discovery, each insight, each revelation of a child being forced to watch her mother deteriorate and die, and then face the world alone, it felt like the weight of a lifetime was lifting from my shoulders.

I could finally see myself—first as a child, then a teen, and then a young adult who had been forced to put her needs and growth aside to survive. I had hidden her away for so long, angry and frustrated at her mistakes, embarrassed by her methods of coping and her codependency. Now, I was immersed in empathy for her. It was like the amount of grace I could have been giving myself all along was proportionate to how much I believed I was worthless. I now understood why the emotions stayed locked up. They were big and scary and would've swallowed me whole. Even today, with all the emotional safety I had brought to the table, the weight of those experiences was still almost too big to shoulder. The younger version of me had done an incredible job of forming resilience and keeping me safe.

Through this discovery journaling, I realized I had been judging younger me from my current perspective instead of loving her for surviving. I had been doing the same to the people in my life—resenting them for not saving me the way I needed to be saved. And then it hit me: that was the problem. No one would ever know how to save me except me. My pattern of attracting and trusting people who would never see, understand, or acknowledge my needs stemmed from the fact that I had been doing the same to myself.

I felt the grief being processed physically—unfamiliar, yet freeing sensations. After weeks of it, I felt lighter, but also emotionally drained. Eventually, the high of releasing so much grief wore off. It started to feel repetitive and depressing. At the same time, I was reading a book about memoir writing. The author spent pages discussing how memory is subjective, and that's when the next answer came: our memories are stories our brains craft to reinforce something, replaying them over and over. My experience was true because it was my experience, but what if I could change the way I viewed it?

As I processed my trauma, I kept thinking, *If only I knew then what I know now*, or *If only someone had been there with my current perspective, my life would be different. But memory is just memory, right? Why not go back? I'm here now, my memory is here now, and my nervous system can't tell time. What if I go back and rewrite the memory? Could changing the story in my mind change how I feel?* Now that I knew what had been hiding in there, I needed to go back and save my younger self.

I remembered an earlier exercise where I visualized going back into a childhood memory as my current self and meeting my younger self there, taking her with me. It had been a powerful demonstration of how memory and visualization work. So, I decided to build on that.

I picked a significant memory from my journaling. After my mom died, I wrapped up her estate, sold all of her (our) things, sold her (our) house, and moved permanently into my college apartment across the state. Until recently, I'd told that story as a badge of honor—focusing on productivity and resilience as the main takeaways. Now that I had looked back, let out the suppressed emotions, felt my way through those two weeks, and allowed my senses to feel what I was too in shock to feel then, it became obvious how that series of practical decisions had upended my sense of safety. That instability had made my nervous system wildly active and in charge, and set me on a path of misaligned life choices. It was a perfect memory to rewrite.

This time, I imagined my current self being there with past me. I asked her what was important. I held space for our grief. I gave her options she didn't know she had back then, and it all flowed out. I would've refused to be *the* receiving line at the viewing—the most traumatic experience of that entire time. I would've delegated more of the funeral planning responsibilities. I would've protected my energy. I would have kept the house. I would have pushed off summer classes. I would have stayed home that summer to grieve. I would have felt what it was like to live in my house without cancer. I would have leaned on my childhood support system. I would have given myself time to go through my mom's things instead of frantically purging them. I would have never had an estate sale in my front yard. I fast-forwarded through the whole summer, imagining a different outcome. I likely would have recognized how unhappy I was at college and transferred closer to home—the home that would've still been there had I not sold the house. I wouldn't have abandoned my own life; I would've helped myself realign it.

With each decision—clear expectations, no urgency, lots of empathy, and space to hold for a traumatized nineteen-year-old—I cared for her like no one else could. I saw her grief and her pain. I anticipated and acknowledged her needs. I cut through her performance, penetrated her walls, and saved her. *I saved her.*

As I wrote, my body responded. Waves of relief washed over me, sending chills down my spine, untangling knots in my stomach, letting air fill my lungs fully. My heart opened. These sensations encouraged me to go deeper into the love and empathy my younger self had been missing. My entire being shifted, and a sense of safety washed over me. I sat in it, I relished it, and for the first time in years, I felt the ground steady beneath my feet. Something monumental had just happened.

The next morning, I woke up feeling like a different person. The only way to describe it—as if I had been walking around missing a vital organ, and that morning, I woke up with it fully functioning. I felt whole in a way I never had before. Writing an alternate memory, filling in the emotional, physical, and financial stability I had lacked, allowed me to feel safe. This sense of safety brought me a type of peace I hadn't known before. It was like the world had slowed down; things felt more quiet, but also more vivid. I felt like I could see clearer and I wasn't constantly on high alert. I stopped actively scanning for problems, and just...existed.

The whole experience felt so surreal I questioned if it had even happened at all. But I knew how I felt that day was markedly different than how I had felt before. I wanted to use my new tool again. As I built emotional stamina, I continued this exercise with other memories—key moments of trauma, grief, or abandonment. The more I showed up for myself, the more complete I felt. Between processing old grief and rewriting my story, my nervous system finally released its hold. For the first time, my brain and body agreed—I was safe.

Now, walking around as someone who felt safe, I knew I could do it again, for the things I would face today or even in the future. I had healed a reoccurring wound at its root.

BECOMING MY FUTURE SELF

My newfound sense of safety felt like a new drug. I rode the high for weeks, watching the effects of this shift unfold. Armed with this sense of security, I felt confident enough to believe in a new future. For the first time, I felt the urge to rejoin the world, building on a foundation that would help me step away from old, repeating patterns. An innate sense of optimism began replacing the willpower-driven survival mode that had consistently left me depleted.

Still, I knew my journey wasn't finished. While I'd tackled my grief and lack of safety, my shattered self-worth remained. Morning pages began to unearth fresh fears, all of which I traced back to limiting beliefs that supported feeling unworthy. The disappointment hit hard, like a setback just as I was gaining momentum.

The tool had moved mountains in my healing, but couldn't rewrite an entire childhood. I needed something else. I was led back into the law of attraction and it's sort of "fake it till you make it" premise. Coming from a newfound sense of safety, I felt more confident I could lean into these teachings.

To become your future self, you just have to believe you're already there. But how do you feel something you've never experienced? How could I pretend to be someone with unshakable self-worth when I had no idea what that felt like? It was a frustrating paradox—*to become healed, I had to believe I was already healed.*

I needed a tangible example. If I could just see it, I could figure it out. After coming up short searching for definitions and stories about people with high self-worth, I turned to ChatGPT. I asked for a story about a forty-year-old-woman who had always had high self-worth—enter Clara.

Clara, a vibrant and accomplished woman, had a childhood brimming with warmth, where curiosity and self-expression were encouraged. Her parents were emotionally available, provided her with a safe environment, and consistently reminded her of her intrinsic worth. Her teachers admired her enthusiasm for learning, and she was known for her kindness and intelligence amongst friends. She had been taught that self-respect and compassion were the foundations of a fulfilling life. I hated her immediately.

Curious for more detail, I asked: "Can you give me an example of her parents empowering her as a child?" Clara had a challenging school project that overwhelmed her. Her parents noticed her anxiety and offered her their comforting presence. They guided her with love and encouragement, holding space for her to learn and grow. Ugh, they sensed and anticipated her needs—I hated all three of them now.

I stewed in jealousy for a little and then erupted in judgement and defensiveness—*Clara was coddled into self-worth*, I told myself. Whereas I'd had to fight and overcome really hard challenges to succeed. Even a therapist had told me I was extraordinary (I justified). I had made this my entire personality for a period of time. College application—look what I had overcome. First job interview—look how mature and capable I was already. I couldn't relate to her at all. People like her felt unreachable, their safety nets so secure that I couldn't see myself in their experience. Deep pain and suffering drew me like a magnet—if I couldn't sense those things in someone, they weren't for me. I needed to tear her down.

"Tell the same story, but her parents are emotionally unavailable," I prompted.

Now Clara's parents were busy, preoccupied with work, and told her, "You'll figure it out," when she asked for help. She was left to navigate her project alone. *Yes, this is better*, I sighed in relief. In this version, Clara figured things out but was marked by an internal struggle to validate her own worth without external affirmation. Now I was rooting for her. Clara became someone I could relate to, someone whose resilience came in response to abandonment.

There it was—Clara and I were the same now, because I had broken her. I read it again: "Clara's journey was marked by an underlying struggle to validate her own worth and achievements without external affirmation." Burn. I realized I was aggressively holding the belief that my resilience was better because it was born from struggle. That belief had helped me survive, but I didn't want to just survive anymore. The truth is, neither Clara nor I was actually broken. We were just doing our best, faced with our circumstances. I was ready to evolve past that fight. I wanted to live freely, without the remnants of a trauma response following me around, and I refused to believe anymore that suffering was the path to acceptance and joy.

I knew what I had to do next. It was time to embrace that my coping mechanisms weren't a badge of honor—they were now hurting me. Once I acknowledged the harm I was doing to myself, I'd be able to shift everything.

I went on to study the qualities that work together to create a foundation of self-worth—resilience, self-acceptance, healthy boundaries, self-compassion, authenticity, achievement and competence, healthy relationships, gratitude and mindfulness, and purpose and meaning.

My next question: "What about someone who has developed similar qualities through trauma response and survival tactics?" The response: "While someone in survival mode can exhibit qualities that resemble resilience or strength, these traits are often reactive rather than proactive. The underlying driver is fear, self-preservation, and unresolved trauma, rather than a deep belief in their own worth. Without self-worth, these survival tactics can become exhausting and limiting, trapping the individual in cycles of anxiety, burnout, or unhealthy relationships. Healing requires shifting from survival-based coping mechanisms to more intentional, self-worth-based living."

I sat stunned. My entire life distilled down to one paragraph. But here I was—I had excavated down to the core. It was in this moment that I could finally see exactly how to make the change.

I studied the coping mechanisms: survival mode, perfectionism/people-pleasing, walls or lack of boundaries, harsh self-criticism, hyper productivity/overachieving, codependency/isolation, hyper-vigilance.

Then I lined them all up. Where I was using perfectionism and people-pleasing to feel worthy, I could shift to self-acceptance. This would require me to let go of my own impossible standards and need for external approval and without judgement embrace my entire self, independent of external achievements or others' opinions. I realized, I had just spent several days making myself my own main-character. I was already doing this!

To the next one—instead of hyper productivity and over-achieving, I'd move to achievement and competence. Meaning, my performing to feel valuable was leaving me exhausted and un-fulfilled. Instead, I could focus on achievement as the process of growth and learning rather than reaching a specific goal or mile-stone. I could do this by leaning into the journey of overcoming challenges, developing skills, and expanding understanding. *Wait! Didn't I just tackle this as I eased into becoming a beginner again?* Moving to competence would be built on the confidence to engage in life's challenges instead of scanning for threats. I would need to trust my ability to figure things out as I go. I already had this skill; I just needed to align my mindset.

The whole thing was really about changing from a fixed mind-set to a growth mindset—which, after reflection, I had plenty of experience in. I knew my underlying drivers were fear, self-preservation, and unresolved trauma—which I had been address-ing for some time now. It turned out, my journey of shifting to self-worth was well underway.

Then I thought back to Clara. I had broken her with a few quick key strokes. But what I was defending? My identity, wrapped up in a trauma response. That wasn't what I wanted anymore. In fact, I'd just uncovered a deep sense of empathy for the younger version of me who had coped that way. I didn't need to defend her anymore; I could thank her, love her, and give myself permission to evolve into the safe, loved, and inherently worthy woman I am.

My test—go back and befriend Clara before I broke her. I re-read her story from a grounded, loving place of self-acceptance, knowing I'm already well along my path of transformation. I discovered a connection between our childhoods, from before my parents divorced. It wasn't all death and drama; there was a foundation of love, safety, and security there. I just hadn't allowed myself to go back to it. I also found similarities between how she was raised and how I now parent my children—and myself. This was huge. I no longer felt the need to defend myself. In fact, I saw myself as both hurt and healed—the vast experiences of my life somehow integrated into something I inherently loved.

Bingo.

It was time to let go of the self-reliant, hard-fought resilience. I had done so much already to even have the courage or ability to leave my old life. I just needed to wake up and accept how far I'd come. I didn't need to work out of fear that I'd keep struggling to seek support or recognize my own needs. I was already swimming in self-compassion.

This summer, I had come to understand the complex and deep layers involved in healing, with safety as the foundation upon which everything else is built. By safely releasing my grief and acknowledging my trauma by rewriting my past memories, I was able to access a level of security that had always eluded me. Now, I was just doubling down on years of regaining my self-worth.

As I've started to nurture myself the way I longed for in my younger years, I've found that my emotional triggers are not obstacles—they are my guides. They show me exactly where I need to focus my energy to heal.

It feels appropriate, sitting here at mid-life, acknowledging the journey that got me to this place. I come back to the word "complete." That part is complete. The road map I crafted for a new type of life relies on nothing more than just doing it. There's that tarot card with the woman standing bound in a puddle. She's not actually bound or drowning—she's just in a puddle. That's me. I just needed to step out.

Now, I walk with a sense of groundedness I didn't know was possible and the knowledge that I am worthy of the life I desire—not because I survived, not because I fought for it, but because I am enough. And for the first time, I believe it.

| 11 |

Brand New

These shifts at my core took practice to fully integrate. Each day, I wake up feeling transformed from who I was just a few months ago, yet incorporating these changes into my daily life still requires intention. I created a tool—a life board—to memorialize this shift and serve as a guide for future choices. As I've crafted a new career path, I've turned to it often. The world isn't built for slow, intuitive, intentional living; it's a chaotic ocean that can easily pull you under if you let it. Every time my intuition raised its hand, I made a point to stop, journal my thoughts and feelings, and then turn to my life board to identify any misalignment.

Each time, it showed me exactly where my steps were drifting from what I truly wanted. My life board became a centering tool and a source of permission to reassess. It's a simple piece of paper divided into four sections: purpose, fulfillment, health, and love. Each section holds a clear vision of how I want my life to feel. When I look at it, I'm reminded of the version of me who crafted it. I'm grateful to her for distilling so much work into a single page of alignment to keep me grounded as I move forward.

As I think back to the beginning of this journey, I remember the mix of emotions: relief from dismantling the final pieces of my old life, pride for how far I'd come, and frustration from a lack of clarity about what was next. There was a moment, sitting on my porch in the summer sun, tears of frustration spilling over as I cried out, "Someone, just tell me what to do."

What I didn't fully realize then was that the person I was asking was myself—because I had the answers all along. I simply needed to listen. By surrendering to the knowledge that I am my own guide, I found the freedom I had been praying for. How liberating it is to realize that we are both our own poison and antidote. Like other great stories of self-discovery, I didn't need to travel the world or meet a guru for answers. I found everything I needed in the ordinary moments of my life—between kids' sports practices and paying bills. I healed by deciding I was worth more than the tolerable suffering I had once accepted.

Here's the thing—the happily ever after is finding my own soul. I looked straight into my own eyes, addressed the things I was scared of, and as I said out loud to myself one day, "Holy shit—the way forward really is through."

For as long as I can remember, I had been avoiding myself and instead searching for a place, a person, a cause to save me—to take me in, validate me, and give me direction. I had also been waiting for my parents to un-abandon me (which is crazy—one of them is literally dead. Don't get me started on my journey through mediumship). And when I looked my fears squarely in the face with the time, space, and compassion that I deserved, I found every single answer I had ever been looking for. They were all coming from me. I didn't need anybody to save me. I needed to save myself.

In its simplest form, the answers lie in attention, focus, perspective, habits, and behaviors. Addressing each of them, ensuring they are in alignment with not only each other, but what you desire, is the road map for change. Then, once you do that, it becomes evident where you're blocked, and it's time for a deep dive into beliefs and core wounds. When I could clearly see my limiting beliefs, and how obviously they were holding me back, I could give them the attention required to lead me right into the face of my core wounds—and from there, elicit fundamental change.

Making changes to the core of who you've been is remarkably energy-consuming and intense. It demands a true desire to chart a new path, and unless you're fully committed to disruptive growth, it might not be for you. Once you shake yourself at your core, you wake up viewing the world you've created differently, reassessing every single choice that the "old you" made. Since I was on the other side of my life-altering decisions—grateful for the courage it took to let go of things that no longer fit, despite not knowing exactly where I was heading—the shift felt more tolerable.

What's waiting on the other side of this transformation is everything you've ever wanted, even if you didn't know it. The best way I can describe it is as a feeling of being fully grounded in knowing. I was once committed to checking every box and hitting every milestone on society's road map to happiness—only to realize that map wasn't meant for me at all (or women, for that matter, but I digress)—there's nothing like the gift of transformative healing I experienced this summer. It has allowed me, at last, to relax into who I truly am and feel confident enough to color outside the lines.

I can't wait to explore new relationships, and revisit old ones. I can't wait to try my skills and creativity at new ventures, and follow my intuition into projects that align with who I truly am. I can't wait to quit things when I feel like I'm done with them, and be proud of how my excitement leads me on the right path, every time. I can't wait to remind myself every single day that the present is the finish line. What I feel now is what matters. There's no right answer at the end of this except the stuff that feels good. That's it. It's that simple.

I'm not scared of the feelings anymore. Jealousy is pointing me toward what I want. Anger is protecting my boundaries. Contrast is helping me craft where I want to go, and pain is alerting me to what needs my attention. All of these things are gifts, not punishments. The rest of it is gratitude, joy, and excitement. How simple is it to just be happy?

It doesn't matter what I do next. I have nothing to prove to anyone other than myself. My only purpose is to filter things into my life that bring me the kind of joy I had as a child, dance in the excitement, and then move on to the next thing when I'm done.

The journey isn't over, of course. With each new expansion comes new lessons and fears. But now, I have the tools I need—including the reminder that it's okay to be a beginner. Just as this book serves as "course notes" to help you speed up your own learning, I created my own tools to guide me when I need them. And I captured all of them in a workbook for you in case you want to try them on. It's open to evolution, allowing new insights and truths to emerge.

I don't feel like I'm playing hooky from life anymore. I feel like I'm living.

Just as I encouraged you at the beginning of this book to listen to yourself, I'll say it again: everything you need is within you. My hope is that these pages have inspired you to uncover the truths you already know and take the steps toward creating your own magic. Healing is rarely linear, but with every choice you make, you're moving closer to the life you're ready for—the one that called you to pick up this book—the one you deserve.

"The wound is the place where the Light enters you."
—Rumi

Afterword

My new list of beliefs—

- Alone is not scary; it's the answer to becoming full enough to attract the relationships I deserve.
- Creative expression is my purpose from my higher self.
- My world is only my mirror. It's full of all of the clues, messages, tests, and validation I could ever need. It shows me the condition of my subconscious conditioning.
- I am not in control. I am guided.
- I am worthy, loved, creative, and innately deserving of everything good.
- Negativity is only either fear-based conditioning that I can change, or contrast leading me to where I want to be.
- The timing is always right because the present moment is the only thing that's real.
- I am the main character; I chose this path. I'm here to transform and expand.
- The beginning and the end are infinite love.
- I have the power to create whatever reality I believe I deserve.
- My thoughts create my feelings, which are the fuel to change.
- My thoughts are rooted in my subconscious conditioning.
- Self-discovery tools are available to me to connect my mirror and my subconscious conditioning.
- I have the power to shift my own beliefs.
- Existing is enough.

Acknowledgements

Thank you to the people who came into my life and made me question everything I ever knew.

Thank you to my childhood besties, whose lifelong friendships make me feel whole.

Thank you to my draft readers who gave me those last nudges of affirmation.

About the Author

Lauren Michele Fields is a writer, speaker, and mentor with 20 years of corporate leadership experience. She spent her career leading teams, building people-centered strategies, and understanding the human experience—from consumers to team members. Known for her ability to connect deeply and inspire action, Lauren has trained and mentored countless individuals, empowering them to step into their potential.

Her debut book, *Just Tell Me What to Do*, is a raw and relatable guide to midlife transformation, offering people the courage and tools to rewrite the narratives that no longer serve them. Lauren combines her corporate insights with her passion for personal development and shares her personal journey of breaking free from societal expectations, facing deep healing, and creating a life aligned with her truest self.

An unapologetic homebody, Lauren finds joy in concerts and live music, dancing in the kitchen, and hanging out with her teenagers. She's a blanket connoisseur, tea enthusiast, and plant lover who lives for sunrises and sings her feelings (sometimes in song lyrics). When she's not writing or mentoring, Lauren curates her home as a sanctuary for creativity and reflection, blending her love of growth with her passion for intentional living.

Learn more about Lauren and connect:
LaurenMicheleFields.com
Instagram @laurenmichelewrites
Substack @laurenmichelewrites

Light the Path

Did this book resonate with you?

If *Just Tell Me What to Do* helped you see things differently, sparked new ideas, or inspired your next step, I'd love to hear about it. Reviews are one of the best ways to help others discover this book and join the conversation. Your words might be exactly what someone else needs to take the next step in their own transformation.

Share on social:

- Instagram: **@laurenmichelewrites**
- Substack: **@laurenmichelewrites**

Looking for more guidance and support?

Check out the ***Just Tell Me What To Do WORKBOOK***. Featuring the exercises and prompts from *Just Tell Me What To Do*.

My **upcoming courses** will provide step-by-step insights, examples, and reassurance as you continue your transformation. Find these and more at **www.laurenmichelefields.com**